who are the privacy invaders?

THEY ARE:

- ◙ THE CREDIT INVESTIGATORS who go to work the minute you open a charge account or take out a loan . . .

- ◙ THE BANKS who talk too much about your income . . .

- ◙ THE BEHAVIORAL SCIENTISTS who secretly record the sounds of unsuspecting couples in the act of love . . .

- ◙ THE EMPLOYERS with their double-barreled application forms, lie-detector tests, psychiatric interviews, neighborhood checks, and security clearances . . .

- ◙ THE EXECUTIVES who spy on employees—tapping telephones, hiring undercover agents, planting microphones and two-way mirrors in the company washrooms . . .

- ◙ THE INSURANCE INSPECTORS and CLAIMS ADJUSTERS whose investigations include secret movies . . .

- ◙ THE CORPORATIONS which play the deadly game of industrial espionage . . .

These are THE PRIVACY INVADERS . . .

> And this is the book that blows the lid off one of the major scandals of our time— a devastating exposé that will hit every American where he lives.

The Privacy Invaders

by Myron Brenton

A CREST REPRINT

FAWCETT PUBLICATIONS, INC., GREENWICH, CONN.
MEMBER OF AMERICAN BOOK PUBLISHERS COUNCIL, INC.

PRINTING HISTORY
Coward-McCann edition published March 13, 1964
Second printing, March 1964
Third printing, May 1964

First Crest printing, November 1964

Crest Books are published by Fawcett World Library,
67 West 44th Street, New York, N. Y. 10036.
Printed in the United States of America.

Acknowledgments

Though this book on our disappearing privacy is credited to me alone, it could not have been completed without the generous cooperation of a great many experts in a wide variety of fields. Unfortunately, a list of their names would be far too long for inclusion here. Each gave willingly of his time and knowledge. In some cases the persons I interviewed were aware that aspects of their work might come in for criticism within these pages, yet this didn't deter them from giving their help. Much assistance—in the form of information, anecdotes and suggestions—came to me from knowledgeable people who requested, however, that they not be identified. Their information, therefore, appears anonymously. My profound thanks to all.

I do owe a special debt of gratitude to William Chiarello, Russ White, Alan Reitman, Jack Hoffman, Toby Reiss and to my editor, Ellis Amburn. Without their many kindnesses my task would have been infinitely harder.

In researching the book I supplemented live interviews with relevant material from books, magazines, newspapers, reports of Congressional and state hearings, privately financed studies, trade journals and pamphlets, as well as other published material. When reference to these sources has seemed to impede the flow of continuity, I have listed them in the Appendix.

Finally, I should state that I alone am responsible for the selection of facts presented herein, for the order in which they appear, and for the conclusions which I have derived from them.

M.B.

TO MY WIFE, HSI-YEN

Contents

1 The Goldfish Age   9

INTRUSION IN THE MARKETPLACE

2 Credit Builds the Goldfish Bowl   17
3 Insurance and Your Privacy   32

INTRUSION AT WORK

4 The Hired Hand . . . and the Hand That Hires   43
5 The Executive File   57
6 The Lie Detector: Industry's Electric Chair, Part One   65
7 The Lie Detector: Industry's Electric Chair, Part Two   76
8 Big Brother on the Job   85
9 IE   100
10 The Electronic Invaders   109

INTRUSION IN THE COMMUNITY

11 Three Community Pressures   126
12 Your Name Is Somebody Else's Fortune   135
13 Fund-Raising and Your Privacy   144
14 In Defense of Privacy   163
Appendix   175

1. The Goldfish Age

*The right to be let alone is indeed
the beginning of all freedom.*
—JUSTICE WILLIAM O. DOUGLAS

HAVE YOU HAD the eerie feeling that you are *not* being let alone? That somebody unknown and unseen is spying on you?

You were not imagining things. Our privacy is up for sale. The intimate details of our lives are being secretly bought, sold, manipulated and exploited by an ever-growing army of private inquirers. They mine our hidden depths, these inquisitive folk, unearthing rich pockets of fact (and sometimes fancy) about our jobs, finances, health, marital relationships, sexual habits and desires, politics, tastes, prejudices and interests. Their prying eyes are everywhere on everyone. What they come up with—and how the information is used—frequently has a profound effect upon our lives. In making their assaults upon our privacy, they are mid-twentieth-century proof that no man is an island—nor free to be one even if he wants to.

Assaults on our privacy? The mind immediately snaps to Big Brother perched on the seat of government. The welfare state, the planned economy, the concentration on internal security generated by the Cold War, the adventures of headline grabbing Congressional investigating committees—all these factors have contributed substantially to the erosion of our privacy. As a result, citizens on both sides of the political balance regularly stage protest meetings, rush to the courts of law, write angry books and seething articles to denounce what they consider unwarranted intrusions into the affairs of citizens. Though William F. Rickenbacker (an editor of the *National Review*) wrote the words that follow to express his bitterness toward the expanded 1960 Census form, they might well sum up the outraged feelings of all champions of privacy in their reaction to all excessive government intrusions.

9

Mr. Rickenbacker stated: "How lush grows the federal jungle! The tentacles of its creepers pierce the walls of all the homes in the land. How can a man be less than outraged by this destruction of his privacy?"

But William Rickenbacker's strangling jungle is only half the story—the half most often and most loudly told. Remarkably little has been said and done about the *private* invaders and exploiters of our privacy—the ones whose main consideration is personal gain, financial or otherwise. Yet their creepers grow with equal vigor and are as dangerous. More so, in fact. In some instances private—and for the most part unpublicized—programs of intrusion have become so excessive they would be considered intolerable were they emanating from governmental circles.

Who are the people so concerned with our personal affairs —concerned enough to pay cash for the information? How do they manage to intrude into areas we thought reasonably safe from trespassers? And what are the ways of fighting back?

This book is an attempt to provide the answers—to identify Big Brother in his civilian clothes. It is an inquiry into the ways in which our private lives are becoming other people's commercial property—in the marketplace, on the job, and around the community. It is a scrutiny into the ways in which private American citizens now spend over $1 billion a year to investigate each other.

Initially perhaps, a rather obvious point ought to be emphasized. We are, most of us, not inclined to be hermits. We don't want to build so high a wall of privacy around ourselves as to be shut off from others. And there is no turning back the clock—which with every tick denudes us further still. The awesome population growth brings an increasing emphasis on organized society. Technological developments speed up the trend to numbered man. A credit economy and a rising theft problem in industry invite all kinds of intrusions. As William Zelermyer, Professor of Business Law at Syracuse University, observes in his penetrating legal study, *Invasion of Privacy*, "Considering the complexities and overpowering demands of current living, privacy assumes the appearance of an imaginary luxury." The point must be conceded: there are "reasonable" encroachments on our privacy, the inevitable price we have to pay for order and progress in the confusing 1960's.

It is the thesis of this book, however, that "reasonable" encroachments are fast becoming unreasonable and irresponsible full-scale invasions, denigrating our privacy to an alarming degree and tending to make intrusion a way of everyday life. Too often, these days, our "inviolate personality," as Justice Louis Brandeis called it, is not only being violated—it is cynically being snatched from us by individuals and institutions who have kidded themselves into believing they have as much right to it as we.

As a result, some ominous things are happening.

We Americans have always been leery of secret files, the trappings of slave states. Yet for the first time the confidential file, the secret dossier, the lists and reports compiled "for subscriber only," are becoming entrenched as an indispensable part of the business scene. As you will see, files have been collected on the personal histories of hundreds of millions of people—exceeding even the burgeoning government collections. Employers, credit and collection agencies, and insurance companies are among the biggest users of such reports. If you are not already the subject of at least one nongovernmental dossier consider yourself a rarity. The day is approaching—and rapidly—when every single adult American, with the possible exception of a few obdurate hill-dwellers and hermits, will find a home in at least one confidential (or, in many cases, not-confidential-enough) file.

This is not to say that dossiers and the investigations that spawned them have no place in the industrial or commercial sphere. In some respects they have become essential. But too often they are collected unnecessarily, excessively—and/or misused. There is also the very real danger that the report may be deliberately slanted to create an unfavorable impression of the subject. The investigative agencies that do the digging have a vested interest in coming up with some dirt. Several investigators in the insurance and employment-background fields have told me they were frankly advised by their agencies to produce a certain quantity of derogatory information. Negative data is, they were informed, the only way a detective agency has of proving its value to its clients. Needless to say, there are investigative agencies that refuse to abide by this self-serving philosophy, but the hazard is there.

Another hazard, just beginning to become apparent, is the growing use of giant computer systems to house all the file information. This trend, implies a Bell Telephone Laboratories official, will provide even greater challenges and problems to privacy in the years to come.

For the first time Americans are required—and required in rapidly increasing numbers—to submit to the ordeal of a lie detector test before being allowed to work. Once the lie

11

test was judged to be an extreme weapon in the police arsenal. Its findings are still not allowed to be introduced as evidence in courts of law. Though its use on applicants for highly "sensitive" positions goes back a number of years, the test is now given to people applying for the most innocuous of jobs in the most ordinary of businesses. Shops, stores, offices and factories from one coast to the other are embracing the lie detector as the final answer to all personnel problems.

In the curious lie detector world, even a person who feels disinclined to try out for a job requiring the polygraph examination is at once suspect. An official of Truth Verification, Inc., a Dallas testing firm, has reported, "About 2 percent of the applicants fail to show up for the test. We have checked on these 2 percent and find that 95 percent of them have some kind of background problem that would have prevented them from getting the job."

The newest, most exotic and futuristic techniques of espionage are being used on a large-scale basis by private individuals. Miniature microphones and recording equipment, wiretaps, closed-circuit TV cameras, two-way mirrors, have all been adapted to private usage—often illegally—by suspicious employers, labor union officials, spouses and others. Some auto dealers are using hidden mikes inside their closing rooms where husbands and wives discuss their imminent purchase of a car in supposed privacy. Jessica Mitford has reported the discovery of a hidden microphone—used to eavesdrop on the private deliberations of the bereaved—inside a prominent undertaker's casket-selection room.

The proliferation of the various spy gadgets is so extensive, their use so varied, that during a Congressional hearing on electronic eavesdropping Senator John A. Carroll of Colorado was moved to explode, "Have we become a nation subject to all these electronic eavesdroppers and wiretappers and 'buggers'? How do we end it?"

The hunt for security risks has become big business as well as being of the utmost consequence to our nation. Making clearance checks on applicants for classified jobs in defense plants, private investigators can—and too often do—allow hearsay, innuendo and the responses of prejudiced informants to creep into their reports. Keeping tabs on the political attitudes and activities of preachers, teachers, scholars, entertainers and millions of ordinary citizens, self-appointed vigilante groups (of both far right and far left persuasion) maintain vast blacklists whose dubious contents are for sale to qualified subscribers. It's hard to resist presenting William Faulkner's pithy remarks about such organizations. The late, renowned novelist said that "in America today any organization or group, simply by functioning under a phrase like Freedom of the Press or National Security or League Against Subversion, can postulate to itself complete immunity to violate the individualness . . . of anyone who is not himself a member of some organization or group numerous enough or rich enough to frighten them off."

The demand for private "intelligence" of all kinds has created a huge army of sleuths, spies, and just plain snoopers. And the army is growing: in 1961, for instance, 675 licensed private detective agencies operated in New York State alone. Within two years the number had jumped to 822.* Elsewhere in the nation the expansion has been similar. There are general investigative agencies, insurance inspectors, credit checkers, auto repossessors, shopping services, security consultants, missing persons bureaus, patent-infringement specialists, bill collectors, divorce detectives and industrial pirates. Innumerable large industrial plants have their own well-paid and well-equipped security staffs. The banking, transportation, thoroughbred racing, perfume and taxicab industries maintain investigative specialists, as do other fields. One small group of highly specialized investigators is active in political investigations, digging up or squashing potential scandals in the Democratic or Republican Party (depending on which is the client, of course). These specialists also nose into the lives of government officials on behalf of private contractors doing business with the government, and perform other chores of a "sensitive" nature.

All of this makes it obvious that investigators play a far more prominent role in your life than the private eye of mystery novel and TV melodrama fame would suggest. If the investigator has the proper contacts—meaning well-placed individuals whom he can bribe or trick—he can get such supposedly confidential information as Western Union messages, unlisted telephone numbers, hotel registration cards, even Social Security and Civil Service records. Even without contacts he can skim off the wealth of private facts you pour throughout your lifetime into the public files. Birth certificates, wedding licenses, car registrations, court records, deeds, mortgages, business licenses, voters' registrations, bankruptcy

---

* Patrol and guard services are included in these figures, but form a small portion of the total.

records and naturalization papers are all public documents.

What you did in school is becoming increasingly important to the people who intrude on your privacy. Both private and government investigators are besieging high schools, colleges and universities for information about past and present students. This inquisitiveness is giving headaches to school administrators who must decide how much information is properly relinquished. It is giving nightmares to those educators who view with alarm the dangers involved in any violation of confidentiality.

The exploitation of our privacy does not end with the prying that takes place in the schools, of course. Gossip and scandal offer a profitable sideline to a segment of the publishing industry. Hidden cameras whirring away on behalf of Madison Avenue catch unsuspecting housewives in action at the local supermarket. The most blatantly intrusive techniques of advertising, pressure and manipulation are being applied in a field whose very basis for existence should preclude such invasions of privacy—the field of philanthropy. Too often, in the wild scramble for your charity dollar and your services as a volunteer, in the frantic effort to squeeze the last drop of the milk of human kindness from your heart, the dignity of the donor is being forgotten. Forgotten or dismissed by the application of the always-specious argument that the end justifies the means.

Sometimes it seems as though your very name no longer belongs exclusively to you. Nor, in fact, *does* your name belong to you alone. You must share it with the $5-billion-a-year direct mail advertising industry which will buy, sell and trade it *ad nauseam*, topping off the piracy by stuffing your mailbox with what has become commonly and understandably known as "junk mail."

If not even your name belongs to you alone, what does? With that question we come full circle to Mr. Justice Douglas's comment at the start of this chapter about the relationship between privacy and freedom. Though we tend sometimes to forget it, the relationship is a deep and personal one. The employees of an eastern aircraft factory that installed 39 hidden microphones throughout the premises are hardly able to call themselves entirely "free." The applicant for an executive position, who must submit to a psyche-dissecting personality test while being secretly investigated by private detectives hired by his prospective employer, is hardly in a position to call his soul completely his own. Life, a wag has said, is like a goldfish bowl. But the question may fairly be raised: who wants to be a goldfish?

It is ironic that so many privacy invasions are launched from the business scene, because business itself is understandably agitated about the infusions emanating from the government. It is further ironic because privacy, as Professor Zelermyer aptly remarked to me, "is concomitant with free enterprise, with competition. Privacy says, 'This is mine.' It gives a person something to call his own." That something is, of course, his individual and unique self. The decline of privacy, then, is in significant measure the story of the decline of individualism.

It was in affirmation of the individual that the concept of privacy as a legal right was first established in the U.S. The year was 1890, the lawyers were Samuel Warren and Louis Brandeis, their vehicle was the *Harvard Law Review*, and their initial motivation was the excessive invasions of privacy committed by the gossip-mongering tabloids of the time. Every person, proclaimed the two attorneys in their trailblazing article, has the right to protect "his private life, which he has seen fit to keep private," the right to his acts and attitudes, the right to "the immunity of the person, the right to one's personality."

That concept, never before enunciated, became the springboard for the recognition of privacy as a legal right in the various states of the Union. Recognition has come neither easily nor painlessly. One judge has described the condition of our privacy laws as still "that of a haystack in a hurricane." There are two basic legal approaches to the right of privacy. The New York approach consists of a statute outlawing the unauthorized use of names, portraits or pictures of living persons in advertising and trade. The Georgia approach, much broader, consists of a judicial decision holding that privacy is derived from natural law—that it is, in effect, an inalienable right guaranteed each individual. Utah and Virginia have followed New York's lead; in nineteen other states the right exists by judicial decision. A number of states have not come to terms with privacy at all.

Insofar as many of the privacy invasions to be discussed on the following pages are concerned, existing statutes and decisions offer little or no protection. Though efforts are being made to find new approaches to the right of privacy, particularly in the light of advancing technology, privacy laws can only go so far before they begin to interfere seriously with other rights—such as those guaranteeing free speech.

15

Much of the intrusion taking place today must come under the heading of a moral, rather than legal, problem.

There is perhaps no better example of the dangerous changes wrought by the climate of intrusion under which we have begun to live than in the investigative phenomenon known as the "neighborhood check." Each day thousands of private, credit and insurance investigators ring thousands of doorbells to ask people the most intimate questions about their next-door neighbors—*and largely get the answers.*

Early in 1963 the *Saturday Evening Post* printed a letter from a woman, clearly an elderly lady, who said that in her day people didn't ask questions and didn't pry. She was unable to understand why things have changed. In point of fact that fine old American expression, which was at once emphatic and had in it an element of dignity—the expression that went, "It's none of your business"—has disappeared from our collective lexicon. Summing up this tendency of ours to carry tales is the following candid remark, made to me by one investigative agency's account executive: "People love to talk about their neighbors. We capitalize on this human failing. We couldn't operate without talkative neighbors." He went on to add, "And neighbors know a hell of a lot more than people realize."

Know, guess, or—as sometimes happens—deliberately lie? But that is a secondary consideration. The moral issue here is paramount. What about this business of talking to strangers about the private lives of those who live nearby? Basically, is it anything but informing?

Naturally, talkative neighbors don't consider themselves informers. The word has a loathsome sound and we associate it with totalitarian nations where tattling like nasty children has been promoted as some higher good. Yet in our ordinary, everyday lives the practice has unwittingly been stealing up on us, too. Often, it must be said, the tattling seems quite innocent. A nice young man comes to Mrs. A's door, asks a few questions about the behavior and activities of Mr. X down the street. It is all very casual and Mrs. A. doesn't want to be rude. But informing it is.

So much for the overall view of the privacy invaders, how they operate, and how they affect us as we stand on the threshhold of what might be called the Age of the Goldfish Bowl. Time now to look at the specifics.

Intrusion
in the
Marketplace

2. Credit Builds the Goldfish Bowl

IF YOU ARE like 100,000,000 other Americans, you began the process of losing your privacy the day you first opened a charge account, took out a loan, bought something on the installment plan, or applied for a credit card. For credit is not, as has been so often suggested, a supreme act of faith on the part of the merchant or banker who extends it. Less ennobling but more to the point, it is a way of doing business that relies on probabilities. The prospective creditor thinks it probable that you will live up to the terms of your agreement. He arrives at this decision only after as much of your personal and financial history has been unearthed as he (or his credit bureau) deems necessary. A man's home may be his castle, as the English are fond of saying, but in a credit economy it cannot help but be built along goldfish bowl specifications.

Precisely what kind of questions about you are asked—and who supplies the information? How is the data handled as to relevancy and confidentiality? Exactly what kind of wheels begin to turn the first time you scrawl your name across the bottom of a credit application form?

The details might surprise—and possibly disturb—you.

To start with, your prospective creditor got in touch with the local credit bureau and ordered a report on you. Because none existed an investigator was assigned to the case. He made a series of information-gathering telephone calls. The first was to your bank. He learned the amount of your average balance, how long you maintained the account, and whether you were a "satisfactory" depositor who had not been tagged with notices of insufficient funds.

Contrary to popular belief, banks—the commercial variety, at least—do talk. They avoid giving exact balances but offer them in round numbers, like "low three figures," meaning $100 to $300, or "high four figures," meaning $7000 to $9999. Savings banks are more circumspect. Usually they refuse to give out any financial data pertaining to their depositors.

Next the investigator called your employer. Almost all companies will give out *some* information on their people. Most reveal how long the employee has been on the payroll and the nature of his job. Some offer personal information such as home address, marital status and number of dependents. The majority verify salary if the investigator quotes a figure, and will say so if the credit applicant has greatly exaggerated his income. Many also slip the word about employees who have been garnisheed.

After talking with your employer, the investigator checked with an informant in the local courts or thumbed through his own files to see if you had any business failures, bankruptcies, mortgage foreclosures, suits or judgments placed against you. Many larger credit bureaus maintain separate court record departments. These do nothing but compile names of litigants and defendants appearing in the local courts. The Credit Bureau of Greater New York has such a division with reports on 14,000,000 suits, judgments and other actions culled daily from the courts of Greater New York and northern New Jersey. The Bureau also publishes the *Daily Litigation Bulletin*, a melancholy sheet that lists all commercial lawsuits newly launched in the area.

Using the telephone or making a field trip, the investigator next interviewed the landlord or superintendent of your apartment building, or—if you lived in a one-family dwelling—your next-door neighbors. These sources told him how long you had resided in the neighborhood, whether they considered you financially responsible, how well you got along with your spouse, and if there was any criticism of your morals, habits or class of associates. He also tried to find out if you were afflicted with a physical or mental illness that might affect your ability to earn a living—and to pay your bills. In one instance a San Francisco woman casually told a credit investigator about her neighbor's short period of mental illness. The neighbor was a married man with several children, trying to swing a loan to establish himself in a small business. He failed to get the money because of the illness the investigator had uncovered.

Somewhere along the conversational path, the investigator might also have learned whether you owned any assets other than your bank account and income. This information would be valuable later should you renege on your payments. Many credit bureaus also operate collection agencies.

If any derogatory information is developed, the investigator double-checks it—or should. A Manhattan credit checker told me how he verified the accusation—made by a neighbor—that a man wanting to make a sizable installment plan purchase was a heavy drinker.

"None of the other neighbors would corroborate the accusation," he recalls. "So I made the rounds of the bars close to where the guy lived. I went in posing as his old G.I. buddy. 'Has my pal been around lately?' I asked the bartenders. Sure enough, that credit applicant hung out every night in one of the bars—and stayed till closing time."

We will assume, however, that in your case not a shred of derogatory information was developed. In that event, the entire collection of facts, opinions, gossip and hearsay was typed and submitted to the merchant or lender who ordered it.

But your story is not yet over.

It is not over because in all probability the credit bureau that handled the probe was a member of the Associated Credit Bureaus of America. The Association is composed of 2,006 credit bureaus and 1,916 collection agencies. Together, these bureaus form a gigantic investigative cloak that covers every square inch of the entire fifty states as well as much of Europe and all of Canada. On Americans alone, Association members collectively maintain files on an awesome number of consumers—120,000,000 of them, according to an ACB of A estimate. As Hillel Black has noted in his critique of credit buying, *Buy Now, Pay Later,* this is "possibly more information on more people than has been collected by the Federal Bureau of Investigation and the Central Intelligence Agency combined."

But there is an even more amazing feature of the ACB of A. *Though Association members are autonomous, they all have access to each other's files and routinely exchange information.* They provide approximately 7,500,000 interbureau reports annually.

What all this means to you is obvious. The minute you

sign for credit you set into motion a sequence of events from which there is no escape. A report, once made, might stick to you forever. Regardless of where—or how often—you move, your credit report—good or bad—can follow you with all the tenacity of your own shadow.

By no means are all initial credit reports as comprehensive as the one I have just described. That one would be made if you were, say, taking out a sizable loan or buying an expensive car. Generally, the scope of the investigation depends on the amount of credit applied for. Thus a neighborhood shop or small department store extending a very moderate amount of credit might be satisfied with little more than an employment verification, bank report, and a search through the litigation files.

Once your file is opened, your credit bureau adds to it continually as you expand your credit horizon. The creditors to whom you owe money are not shy. They readily report whether you are fast pay, slow pay, or no pay. If you fall behind in your payments without any kind of explanation the shopkeeper or lender calls the credit bureau on his own initiative to give you away. Some eager-beaver stores hasten to the telephone when a customer is just three weeks behind in his payments. Most are reasonable, waiting three months or so. Once the damning call is made, of course, you will have a tough time getting credit elsewhere—at least until you straighten out your affairs.

Added to the monolithic structure of the ACB of A are several thousand nonaffiliated credit bureaus. A recent survey showed 27 bureaus in the San Francisco Bay area alone. A giant organization in the credit reporting field is the Retail Credit Company, which makes all types of credit and insurance checks and has offices in 1,600 North American cities, including Mexico City and San Juan, Puerto Rico. This firm maintains files on over 42,000,000 persons.

An investigative wrinkle that stands Retail Credit and most other bureaus in good stead is newspaper clips. A file is begun on anyone whose name appears in the paper as a result of an auto accident, drunk driving charge, morals or other arrests, divorce, marriage, inheritance, etc. Yes, quite possibly your name reposes in some local credit bureau even if you never applied for credit.

The proliferation of credit bureaus is beginning to create problems. Not all agencies, it seems, are crackerjack outfits probing every minute detail of the credit applicant's financial history. The reporting has in some instances been sloppy enough to generate a growing rumble of complaints. These come mainly from bankers and from the Federal Housing Administration, which uses credit reports in passing on mortgage loans.

In mid-1963 the *Wall Street Journal* told of an interesting study made by the FHA on 1,237 cases in which it had to take over the mortgage applicant's home. Fully 29 percent of the mortgage applications would have been rejected in the first place, the FHA found, "if the original credit report had not been deficient or inaccurate."

Part of the trouble stems from the surprising fact that there is no state licensing of credit bureaus anywhere in the U.S. (though the ACB of A sets standards for its members). A number of unqualified or actually dishonest people have gone into the business. In some cases a credit bureau employee was fired for incompetence, then opened up his own office in competition with the one that fired him. Such persons might well be open to fraudulent dealings. And there have been recent instances of fraud in the FHA mortgage field—where unethical lenders have paid equally unscrupulous credit bureau owners to *delete* derogatory information from reports that had to be submitted to the FHA, which would guarantee the loan.

By and large, it must be assumed the nation's credit bureaus are ethical and doing a good job. Otherwise government investigators and local police departments would not be using the bureaus' files as much as they do. The ACB of A has stated that the FBI is one of the largest users of credit bureau services. Hillel Black reports that so many government investigators drop by the Credit Bureau of Greater New York each day, the Bureau has even set aside a special table for them.

Some bureaus give their subscribers a kind of blacklist— euphemistically called a list of "danger signals." These are occupations or circumstances that supposedly call for caution on the part of the would-be creditor. One such list, compiled by a New York credit bureau, offers an insight into a field that not only unearths the intimate details of your life but also places value judgments on them.

Is there something about *your* life that would provoke a credit man to flash the amber light of caution? Among the more than 20 factors mentioned are such items as living in a "furnished apartment," impressing the credit grantor with their "extreme desirability as credit risks," claiming to have

21

a good income "which cannot be verified," and not carrying a "regular checking account."

The list also includes "divorced or separated women or widows who cannot supply financial references," and "generally unstable, hazardous or transient occupations such as bartender, dishwasher, taxi driver, longshoreman," among others. Conformity, it seems, is one key to a good credit rating. The Bureau does state that danger signals "must be used intelligently and with good judgment; they suggest caution or careful investigation but are not all definite reasons for refusing credit."

How valid are such lists? The man who drives a taxi and lives in a furnished apartment but is as steady as they come would dispute their validity. So do some of the people in the credit business. The manager of one metropolitan credit bureau, in the credit field for years, refuses to have anything to do with them. Though he declined to be identified, for fear of getting into a dispute with credit men who do use them, he told me emphatically, "I won't pass the lists on to my clients. As generalities, they're unfair. As danger signals, they're unrealistic. Take stevedores. Some have been at their jobs for twenty-five or thirty years. They're steady and reliable. We give the subscriber the facts. What a man does, what kind of a paying record he has. But we let the subscriber make up his own mind about extending credit."

Foreign visitors to our shores—especially those coming from England—are startled by our credit rating system. While credit-buying is a well-established institution in England, the investigative file that sticks like a shadow is not. Most Englishmen who buy on credit simply give their name, address, job reference and age. The information stays with the lender. But some powerful British financial interests have been looking—and looking with increasing admiration—at the American credit bureau. Beset by a rising tide of bad debts, these financiers want to establish a central consumer credit clearinghouse, where everybody in England who buys on the "never-never" would be filed. It will not come to pass without a lot of hand-wringing. As the distinguished English journal, *The Economist,* noted, "The prospect of his financial standing becoming public knowledge is regarded by the Englishman with much the same horror as having his fingerprints filed in New Scotland Yard."

The field of credit reporting has all kinds of intriguing little highways and byways to offer the person not steeped in its lore. Take the comparatively recent but increasingly popular development of tenant reports. These are exactly what the term implies—credit checks ordered by cautious landlords on prospective tenants.

Agencies specializing in this type of investigation have sprung up all over the U.S., particularly in the large urban centers with their wealth of multi-unit apartment buildings and residential complexes, like New York, Chicago and Los Angeles. Long-established investigative bureaus like Retail Credit have also gone on the tenant-check bandwagon. You too might be investigated should you happen to move to a very large apartment building within the next few years. Keeping that fact in mind, you will find it illuminating to look over a typical tenant report form. The questions, of course, apply to the prospective tenant.

1. Years known?
2. Are name and address correct?
3. About what is his age?
4. What is his racial descent? (Not asked in states having antidiscrimination statutes.)
5. Is he married?
6. What is the number of his dependents including wife?
7. Does he have any young children? If so, give ages.
8. Does he keep dogs, cats or other domestic animals on the premises?
9. By whom is he employed?
10. What position does he hold?
11. How long has he been with his present employer?
12. Does he work full-time?
13. Does he conduct his business from his residence?
14. Are his prospects for continued employment good?
15. About what is his annual earned income from his work or business?
16. About what annual income, if any, does he have from other sources such as pensions, investments, contributions, rentals, etc.
17. If married, does his wife follow a gainful occupation? What is her individual annual income?
18. How long has he lived at present address?
19. Does he maintain the premises in good condition?
20. Do you learn that he has ever been dispossessed or sued for nonpayment of rent?
21. Any complaints from other tenants reflecting on his desirability as a tenant?

23

22. What monthly rent does he pay at present?
23. Is his rent paid promptly when due?

I went over these questions with my own landlord. His is a well-kept building containing only two- and three-bedroom units. He is quite careful about his choice of tenants. Yet he felt that questions 14 through 17 and 22 "just are not the landlord's business."

On a couple of informative afternoons I watched some enthusiastic tenant investigators at work. The firm was Robert and Gordon Services, a Manhattan-based bureau run by Gordon G. Duffy and his partner, Frank Alpert. Duffy, a lean, rather intense and surprisingly sensitive man in his mid-thirties, estimates they handle about 40 percent of the tenant applications being investigated in the Greater New York area. This includes apartment houses, cooperatives, and city housing projects. (The firm also makes mortgage and related reports.) Some clients are the Lefrak Organization, the largest private builders in the U.S.; Webb & Knapp, a well-known building firm; and Herbert Charles & Co., a very successful renting and managing agency with offices in several states.

One section of the three-room office is taken up by the investigators, who do much of their checking over the telephone. In New York City, all kinds of directories are available to facilitate telephone investigations. There is a "by-street" telephone directory which lists subscribers by street address rather than by name. Neighbors can be reached through that one. Real estate directories list the landlords of each building in New York's five boroughs. There are also national directories listing professional people, such as doctors and lawyers; these give the date each professional was licensed to practice.

Alpert himself contacts several dozen informants a day and says flatly, "I have never been turned down for information." Like most investigators, he has his own distinct style for dragging intelligence out of reluctant informants. If he were to ask you about the man who lives next door, he would involve you in a long-winded conversation, buddy-buddy style, before you knew it. Where appropriate, he does beautiful impersonations, lapsing into an Italian or Yiddish or other distinctive accent to stimulate rapport.

One of the items this bureau is particularly on the lookout for: earning ability in relation to the rental fee of the apartment. The quest for this information can lead to some weird conclusions. In one case handled by Duffy, a girl earning $80 a week as an office worker wanted to rent a snazzy $225-a-month apartment. The client, a rental agency, was curious about her ability to afford this high-style living. Investigation unearthed the reason she felt on safe financial ground. She was consorting with the owner of the building.

Duffy does not know the outcome of that one. He gave that report to his client over the telephone and never heard any more about it.

Several investigators who do tenant-checking on the eastern seaboard told me they often play down the really intimate stuff if they feel it has no bearing on the rental situations. But others said they include everything that smacks of dirt because, as one manager put it, "If everybody comes out white the clients don't need us." I was to hear this reasoning time and again during the course of my research. Sound reasoning, I might add, from the self-serving point of view. What this means is that it can go either way if an investigator discovers any skeletons in your closet. He can, at his discretion, muffle their rattling bones. Or he can make them click like castanets for the edification of the man who is paying for the report.

Tenant reports serve "useful" purposes perhaps not thought of when they were first conceived. In some Northern cities, landlords reluctant to rent to Negroes sometimes try to manipulate reports to get around antidiscrimination laws. The old gambit, "The apartment's already taken," no longer works so well. But in the Goldfish Age, an effective ploy is, "Your credit application isn't satisfactory," for it implies that the undesirable applicant certainly could have moved in if there hadn't been something wrong with his finances or morals or both. For the ploy to work, of course, something unfavorable must be uncovered. The landlords who work tenant reports this way tell their credit checkers, essentially, "I don't care what you find that's wrong about the applicant. Just find it."

One investigator told me, "I really have to wrestle with my conscience in situations like that. If you dig deep enough, you can find something wrong with everybody." He resolves his dilemma rather uniquely. First he does the client's bidding. Then he informs New York's antidiscrimination agency, the Commission on Human Rights, about the action taken. However, to protect himself he refuses to turn over his records to COHR voluntarily, insisting that they be subpoenaed.

Credit reports, too, have a way of wandering far afield from their original purpose. Though credit reports are "privileged communications," rendering them libel-proof; though they are supposedly confidential and available only to credit bureau subscribers in matters involving contracts and agreements, it would seem that the man on the street hardly faces insurmountable problems in obtaining a credit report on anyone he wants, for any purpose whatsoever. He may find a business friend, a legitimate subscriber, willing to order a report on his behalf. That destroys the "privileged communications" aspect and leaves the parties open to a libel suit by the subject of the report, but plenty of people are willing to take the risk. You can also buy a credit report directly from a bureau more interested in business than ethics. A bureau willing to service a stranger might be difficult to find in the cities, but not in small towns and suburban communities. I tried to purchase reports from five suburban credit bureaus east of the Rocky Mountains, in each case explaining that I contemplated going into partnership with someone but wanted to check up on him beforehand. Only two bureaus refused to sell me a report.

One fascinating non-credit use for credit reports illustrates how democratic the spirit of investigation has become. Time was when only the extremely wealthy would hire private detectives to work up background reports on their daughters' prospective bridegrooms, to make sure the young men were not cads, fortune-hunters or otherwise unsuitable. Now, numerous investigators tell me, the middle class is taking over this practice. Detectives—who frequently charge $50 or $100 a day plus expenses for their services—are still too costly a proposition. But a $5 or $10 credit report will do the trick, and nicely. In one instance a stockbroker forbade his daughter to marry her suitor who, the credit report said, had been fired from two jobs for malingering and was six months past due in paying most of his bills. Another intended marriage fell through when the boy's family discovered, through the credit report, that the girl was twice divorced—a fact which the boy knew but had withheld from them. However, some parents are more interested in their opposites—the parents of the boy or girl their child will marry. They want to find out if—or perhaps make sure that—their offspring is marrying into a family of means. The credit report is a cheap and tactful way of eliciting this intelligence.

Lawyers find a number of uses for credit reports, sometimes even utilizing them to check on prospective jurors. In

26

1958 a U.S. Senate committee looking into improper activities in the labor-management field heard an International Teamsters' Union lawyer admit to the practice. The union had ordered $2 commercial credit reports on prospective jurors in one of Teamsters' president James R. Hoffa's trials. It might not be too farfetched to assume that the Government has made similar use of credit reports when a federal jury is being empaneled. As a matter of fact, the Government has even used income tax returns to investigate prospective jurors. The 1954 trial of Frank Costello on income tax evasion is a case in point. The Government checked jurors' tax records in order to keep off the jury anyone who had income tax troubles of his own. Later, U.S. attorneys were instructed to discontinue investigating jurors because it might have a "bad effect."

Small-town credit bureaus sometimes play fast and loose with their so-called confidential files by selling subjects' names and addresses to mailing list compilers. One successful compiler, Herbert Odza, told me, "Often these bureaus sell separate lists—one of slow-paying, the other of prompt-paying people."

Another example of the way credit information receives far wider application than one might suspect involves a legitimate credit bureau function. Many bureaus furnish not only credit reports but also personnel reports on applicants for employment in their areas. Often the applicant is already the subject of a credit report in the bureau's files. Information from that report goes into the personnel dossier, which means the prospective employer receives a detailed picture of the way the applicant goes about his financial affairs.

Not even the all-pervasive American system of credit ratings can pinpoint all of the people who will, ultimately, default on the payments. The ACB of A estimates that between 1 percent and 2 percent of all credit purchasers are, to use the Association's quaint term, confirmed "won't-pays." These credit delinquents comprise all economic levels, from the debt-ridden slum dweller to the wretchedly overextended owner of a $40,000 split-level. They are targets for the nation's coterie of bill collectors, skip-tracers and repossessors. The vast scope of the U.S. collection business can be seen by the fact that the 2,275 members of the American Collectors Association, an organization that maintains certain ethical standards in its field, alone receive $1 billion worth of claims annually.

In their battle of wits with credit delinquents and professional bill dodgers, ethical collection outfits are cunning and artful—as they should be. They use anxiety-building dunning notes, psychologically oriented interviews, some counseling where applicable, ingenious stratagems to locate debtors who have fled for parts unknown, and persistence, persistence, persistence. But a segment of the debtor-hunting fraternity, going beyond art and artifice, engages in the most pernicious invasions of privacy to accomplish its purpose. This segment justifies itself by pointing to the irresponsibility of actual dishonesty of the individual who does not pay his bills. It is true that many credit delinquents are nothing more than a species of petty swindler. It is also true that many people who do not pay their bills are involved in genuine disputes with their creditors or were victimized by high-pressure credit merchants. But regardless of the background of the particular case, neither the courts nor regulatory agencies have gone along with the idea that the debtor has lost his right to privacy. Significantly, of all the invasion-of-privacy suits launched since the turn of the century, a large proportion concerns the activities of collection agencies.

One illustration of the way a debtor can be hounded—and do something about his plight—involves an Ohio case of a few years ago. The collection agency was attempting to collect, from a schoolteacher, a past-due medical bill. The agency tormented the debtor by telephoning him as much as eight times a day, every day of the week, both at home and at work, from morning until midnight. It telephoned his superiors and told them about the debt. On at least one occasion the collection agency called the debtor at work three times in 15 minutes.

The ordeal—by no means unique in the annals of beleaguered debtors—lasted for three weeks. By then the schoolteacher was close to a nervous breakdown, and on the verge of losing his job. Finally deciding to fight back, he began an invasion-of-privacy suit against the collection agency. The lawsuit reached Ohio's highest court—which ruled in favor of the teacher.

An equally vicious technique was used on a Missouri woman who went to court in 1959. She and her husband purchased some furniture on time and eventually fell behind in their payments because they felt they were not being properly credited for payments already made. The furniture store hired an outside collector. The collector tracked the wife to a café where she worked as a waitress. Loudly, in front of all

28

the customers, he demanded payment. She tried to ignore him. He followed her around, threatened to stay all day, told her he could get her fired. In one of his outbursts he shouted, "Something is going to be done while I am here! I think you're deadbeats. I don't think you intended to pay for the furniture when you got it!" Far from being intimidated, the waitress consulted an attorney. The result was an invasion-of-privacy lawsuit—which she won, collecting damages.

Instances such as these prompted the *Commercial Law Journal* to warn collection agencies and attorneys, "Any method used in attempting to obtain payment of a debt, which tends to impute dishonesty to the debtor, or to expose him to disgrace and ridicule, or to invade his right of privacy gives a right of action for damages to the debtor against the person employing such methods."

Harassment on the part of bill collectors can flourish anywhere, but occurs most frequently in areas where state regulations are weak, poorly enforced or nonexistent. Tragically, many instances of strong-arm tactics never come to light because the unethical segment of the collection industry saves its most pernicious acts for poorly educated debtors and those in the lower income group. The unscrupulous bill collector feels that debtors in these categories are the most easily intimidated and the least apt to make official complaints. When a California Senate Interim Committee, under the chairmanship of the then Senator Fred H. Kraft, began to investigate the activities of bill collectors in 1957, it uncovered numerous examples of intimidation. The Kraft Committee charged some California collection agencies with using "strong-arm and other ruthless methods to force people into paying their bills." Some hapless debtors, threatened with bodily harm, actually hired private detectives as bodyguards to accompany them to collection agency offices. Though bill collectors were licensed by the State, supervision was reported to be lax, resulting in these conditions. Subsequently, the licensing regulations were tightened and enforced.

For years the Federal Trade Commission, Better Business Bureaus and some state police agencies have been concerned about another specialty within the collection field—skip-tracing, the locating of debtors who have fled their last known address. What arouses the most concern, criticism and orders to cease-and-desist are the fictitious forms sent out by professional skip-tracers to trap "skips" into revealing their home address, place of employment, or the name and address of their bank. An hour's browsing through the files of the

National Better Business Bureau gave me numerous examples of the kind of illegal forms that have been popular with unscrupulous skip-tracers. Most were official-looking documents bearing titles strongly suggestive of government agencies, such as "The National Service Bureau," "Department of Disbursements," "Employment Questionnaire," and "National Inheritance Bureau." Many bore an emblem representing the American eagle and all were to be sent to the credit delinquent from a Washington, D.C., mail drop. There were also forms from a phony freight-forwarding company (that purportedly held a package for the debtor), a fictitious Hollywood casting office (wanting to use the debtor as an extra in a movie to be filmed in his town), and a nonexistent pen company offering free samples of its product. In each case, the debtor was instructed to fill out a questionnaire that asked where he lived, worked, banked, and the identity of his closest relatives. Debtors who sent away for the pen company's free sample received an ordinary pen point—value, one cent. In this case, the Government prosecuted the company that manufactured and sold these forms. Noted a U.S. Court of Appeals, "Petitioner's scheme is a cheap swindle and the argument that it is less so because it may in certain cases trap swindling debtors is not one pleasing to entertain."

Skip-tracers also use the telephone to good advantage in obtaining information on the skip's whereabouts or place of employment. The tracer may pretend to line up contestants for a TV show, conduct a market research survey, be an insurance agent checking on some life insurance the debtor supposedly bought, masquerade as a government investigator or welfare official. The disguises are, obviously, only limited by the ingenuity and talent of the tracer. Usually they work best with the debtor's relatives who, in all innocence, blurt out the salient information. Masquerading as a government official is illegal everywhere. Some of the other tricks are frowned upon in a few states, not in others. The National Better Business Bureau finds objectionable any means to collect overdue bills that resorts to "false and misleading artifices," which would seem to take in much of the skip-tracer's repertoire.

One of the least publicized agents in the credit world's police force is the repossessor. This is understandable. Repossession hardly makes for good public relations, even when the victim has clearly defaulted on his credit obligations. The image it conjures up is of a poverty-stricken family standing tearful and bereft in the center of its living room while all around the premises hardened repossessors, unmoved by the family's pleas, carry out the furnishings.

Nevertheless, the repossession business is booming. Repossessors have taken back practically everything that can be bought on time, including such items as TV sets, refrigerators, washers, pianos, automobiles, even wedding rings. Wherever possible, repossessors prefer to remove the item without the debtor's knowledge—and for good reason. Repossessors have been beaten up, shot, stabbed, clubbed, cursed and kidnapped during the course of their appointed rounds. The automobile lends itself most to being taken by stealth. Fortunately for the repossessors, it is also the object most often removed.

A Rhode Island repossessor's method, which is fairly standard, was described by the *Wall Street Journal*. The repossessor and his staff prowl around in radio cars equipped with burglary tools. Within minutes after spotting the vehicle to be repossessed they are inside, jumping the ignition, driving it away. The car is completely intact; and as soon as it has been taken the police are notified.

State laws vary considerably in the leeway given repossessors. Some states do not allow private detectives to undertake repossession jobs. A few do not allow independent repossessors to function at all. In Connecticut, for instance, repossessions are made by a sheriff's deputy or by an actual employee of the finance company, bank or store holding title to the credit item. Many states prohibit repossession of items essential to personal maintenance—though what constitutes "essential" varies from state to state. Repossessors themselves can hardly be expected to advise a debtor of his rights.

Ugly situations can develop when state laws relating to repossessors are weak or their supervision lax. The Kraft Committee in California was especially critical of repossessors. It pointed out that repossession had provided a "hunting ground for petty racketeers, thugs, wildcatters, ex-convicts and musclemen." Witnesses testifying before the Committee told of "invasions of privacy, beatings, illegal breaking and entering, larceny, impersonations of law officers, and many other offenses." As far as the fringe outfits in the credit-collection field are concerned, the credit delinquent has no rights at all —save the one of paying up.

3. Insurance and Your Privacy

IT MAY STARTLE you to learn that you were probably secretly investigated when you first took out (and possible renewed) your auto, fire, burglary, theft, homeowners or life insurance policy. Fully three-fourths of all U.S. policyholders are checked out without their knowing it before issuance of their policies actually takes place. Usually it works like this. When you apply to your agent or broker for insurance, he places you on a "binder." The binder affords temporary coverage, just as long as it takes the insurance underwriter to decide whether you are a poor risk—somebody his company could well do without insuring. To help him in his appraisal he orders an "inspection report"—neat little euphemism, this, for an investigative file that exposes much of your business, personal and financial life. Insurance being a statistical gamble, the inspection report is one way in which the company hedges its bet.

Though these inspection reports are very nearly made on as wholesale a basis as credit checks, there is at least one important difference between the two. Most installment-plan buyers take it for granted they will be investigated; few applicants for insurance have any such notion. One cannot help wondering why insurance brokers, agents and companies are for the most part seemingly reluctant to tell prospective policyholders that their private lives will be scrutinized. Would it make for poor public relations? A Continental Insurance Company official apparently thought not; he told me, "The only people who'll resent investigations are the poor risks."

Biggest insurance inspection bureau in the nation is the Retail Credit Company with 259 branch offices covering 1,600 North American cities. Every year it writes some 12,000,000 reports, a goodly portion of which go to insurance companies. The Hooper-Holmes Bureau, with clients such as Metropolitan Life, Allstate, Prudential and Nationwide, has 138 offices and churns out some 3,500,000 reports annually. O'Hanlon Reports, somewhat smaller, also develops information on millions of insurance applicants yearly. And there are countless one-office bureaus scattered throughout the U.S.

A typical inspection report reveals the extent to which your private life becomes the insurance company's property. The one that follows concerns a Californian who had applied for bodily injury and property damage insurance on a 1960 Chevrolet. The report is completely factual except for alteration of names and addresses.

BUSINESS: John K_____ is employed as a tool-and-die maker by the XYZ Manufacturing Company, 5 Manhattan Lane, Los Angeles, California. He has been so engaged for the past 4 years. His wife occasionally works in a local shop on a part-time basis but is not regularly employed. Assured's financial worth is estimated at $3,500 consisting of personal property and savings. His income is estimated at $5,000 per annum. He appears to live within his income and there is no indication of financial stress.

PERSONAL: Your assured is white, Italian-American, about 38 years of age. He is married and lives with his wife and two children in a duplex apartment at 8750 East Westmoreland Street, Los Angeles, California. This is a lower-middle-class residential section of mixed character; vandalism somewhat higher than average. Assured has resided at this address for the past two years. He is known to drink wine and other intoxicants moderately, but has never been known to drink to excess. He has not been seen driving while under the influence of intoxicants. He is well regarded by his neighbors and there is no criticism of his habits and morals.

CAR AND DRIVER: Your assured drives a 1960 Chevrolet 4-door sedan which was inspected. Car was found to be in good operating condition. Tires have adequate tread, brakes and lights function properly. There is a slight dent in the right front fender, which assured's wife claims was caused by unknown parties in a parking lot. No other signs of damage. Car is garaged at night. Speedometer reading is 10,005 miles. Car bears Calif. license no. CZ_____. Assured drives vehicle to work daily, one-way distance of 12 miles. Annual estimated mileage is around 12,000. Assured is the sole driver of the car; his wife does not know how to drive. Informants state that assured handles a car well, but is considered a fast driver and is criticized for occasionally driving at excessive speeds in this residential section.

DRIVERS UNDER 25: Assured's two daughters are aged 10 and 12. No young driver exposure on this risk.

Loss Record: Assured is not known to have been involved in any accidents or incurred any other losses, and informants know of no moving violations. MVR record attached.*

What about this report? Is it unusual? It is not; tens of thousands like it are written every month (allowing for variations as they apply to other types of insurance). In point of fact, I deliberately chose a somewhat prosaic report. Because it is more typical than sensational, it underscores with even greater force the incursions made into your private life when you buy insurance. But let's dwell for a moment on inquiries that smack more of sensationalism. Not that these are exceptions by any means. In thousands of cases each month, the questions asked—and answered—about the prospective policyholders are appallingly clinical.

For example, when a single, divorced or widowed woman takes out a floater policy on an expensive ring or fur coat, the company is eager to know all it can about her social life. Does she travel a lot? Does she entertain extensively—meaning, does she throw a lot of wild parties? Is there any criticism of her morals—in other words, do men spend the night with her?

When an applicant for auto or life insurance is criticized for drinking, the carriers require inspection bureaus to fill out a special questionnaire, as follows: How often does he drink to excess (daily, weekly, semiweekly, monthly)? To what degree does he drink (gets drunk, stupefied, entirely out of control)? Or is he loud and boisterous but not entirely out of control? How many drinks does he usually take on these occasions? What does he usually drink (beer, wine, whisky)? Where does he usually do his drinking (home, bars, club, etc.)? When was the last occasion of this sort?

Despite the comprehensive nature of the questions, routine insurance inspections are "quickie" investigations. Inspectors are paid on a piecework basis or work on a quota system. A live-wire inspector may polish off 15 or more cases a day. Since each case requires interviewing at least two informants, the live wire rushes through as many as 30-35 people a day. Whom does he see? Inspectors rely primarily on the applicant's employer, neighbors and/or apartment house super (when one is available). In some small towns the local banker

* Every state maintains Motor Vehicle Records on each registered driver. These are public records. Typically, they show violations, convictions, impairments, accidents, limitations, etc.

or chief of police may be willing to provide the necessary data about the applicant, probably rewarded with a bottle of good Scotch at Christmas. Mainly, however, reliance is placed on what the applicant's neighbors have to say. In other words, whether he gets his insurance policy may very well depend on what the neighbors know, think and tell about him.

With the volume of inspection reports growing every year, more people are being questioned about their neighbors than ever before. You too may have an insurance inspector in your future. To the thoughtful observer this system of neighbor-informants provides a source of wonderment. Imagine all the varieties of hell that would be raised if a government agency relied on the blanket use of neighbors to obtain information; say, if the Internal Revenue Service seriously expected each citizen to turn informer and pass judgment on whether the person next door is cheating on his income tax! Yet the insurance companies—through the inspection bureaus —get parallel cooperation.

In actual practice, the neighborhood check has just so much stretching power before it breaks down. Inspectors find that even people willing to spread *some* dirt often balk when the questioning becomes too close and detailed. Yet the reports must be completed. What do the inspectors do? Frequently they rely on guesswork, taking into account the tenor of the interviews they actually did conduct.

There is pressure on the inspectors to slant their reports unfavorably. As the manager of one West Coast bureau explained to an inspector whose output of derogatory reports had been too few in number, "We're in business to find bad risks. If everybody comes out clean, we don't justify our existence." Another manager has pinned a monthly list in a prominent spot on the office wall, ranking each inspector according to the number of derogatory reports he turned in. Inspectors in that office surely need no pep talk in order to slant reports negatively whenever possible.

Inspection reports are occasionally used to screen out groups considered undesirable from the risk standpoint. One inspector told me he was instructed to "be careful" in writing auto reports on Negroes, elderly drivers, and males under twenty-five. He understood that to be an oblique suggestion that he find some derogatory information in those categories. Later several other inspectors in that office were given the same suggestion more directly. When an applicant for auto insurance is labeled a bad risk and denied insurance, he is tossed into a statewide assigned-risk pool. Some other company "draws" him from the pool, but charges a special—and exorbitantly high—rate for the policy.

Insurance companies have the right, of course, to turn down any applicant they wish, without inspection or explanation. But to do so blatantly would engender poor public relations and offend brokers. The companies try not to offend their brokers. In fact, until comparatively recently, inspectors were not permitted to interview applicants directly because brokers looked upon this practice with disfavor. On some lines of insurance, applicants are still not approached directly. Oddly, brokers as a group do not seem to mind clandestine investigations of their clients.

The most exhaustive, penetrating reports of all are made on applicants for high-priced life insurance and, in some cases, on applicants insuring extremely expensive jewelry, furs, art objects, and the like. Sometimes these comprehensive reports are made by an insurance company's special agents or by a private detective. I saw one report prepared by a detective. It was a memorable dossier, made for a life insurance company on a titled member of the jet set currently living in New York City. The report left nothing to the imagination. It detailed the reason he married (his wife was quite wealthy). It alluded to his diverse sexual activities. It broke down his income into its component parts—salary, dividends, interests, rents. It described his wife's assets and commented on future financial prospects. It also described his wife's uninhibited social activities in New York City and elsewhere. This report was perhaps exceptional for its lurid content, but in its scope and detail it did not vary from other inspection reports of its kind. They are remarkably thorough and would do an FBI file proud. Indeed, the FBI and other governmental investigative agencies have full access to insurance inspection reports.

The avalanche of claims descending on the nation's insurance companies each year has prompted the creation of a vast investigative network of which inspection bureaus are one small part. Every major insurance company has its own staff of claims adjusters and highly trained investigators. Many of the latter are former FBI agents. The industry as a whole has a number of important associations, each with its own investigative arm. The National Theft Bureau, the Fire Underwriters' Arson Department and the Claims Bureau of the Association of Casualty and Surety Companies are three prominent examples. A number of private detective agencies, like Pinkerton's National Detective Agency, Inc., are also used by some companies to work insurance claims. In addition, the insurance industry has built up huge permanent files of claimants, kept in central clearinghouses for use of all member companies. The "Index System" is a clearinghouse for personal injury claims records; in 1962 it had 16,704,266 claims on file. The Casualty Index, manned by the Hooper-Holmes Bureau, serves some 110 accident and health companies and has accumulated more than 6,500,000 claims files. These files pinpoint habitual or professional claimants whose claims are likely to be exaggerated or totally fraudulent.

Is all this frantic intrusion into the affairs of claimants really necessary? The answer is not to be found in the insurance ads depicting the friendly claims man who renders a speedy and eminently fair settlement on behalf of the friendly claimant. In reality, mutual and justifiable suspicion often sets the tone for the claims negotiation. The insurance company looks at the claim with the wary eye of a housewife cheated once too often at the checkout counter. The claimant files his claim with the embittered mien of a person sure he will get a raw deal and determined to do something about it.

These conflicting attitudes are particularly prevalent in the case of automobile claims, of which there are an astronomical lot each year.* N. Morgan Woods, courtly and affable manager of the Claims Bureau, has not been hesitant in voicing his opinion about the integrity of claimants: "Based on my twenty years of observation and experience in insurance investigations," he has stated, "I would estimate that about 75 percent of the automobile and general liability claims are tainted with some aspect of fraud."

Personal injury claimants of course have a slightly different view. Their attitudes were the focus of a three-year study by Columbia University's School of Law. Reporting on this study, the insurance trade journal, the *National Underwriter*, stated that claimants "believe that the insurance companies have received large sums of money as premiums over the years, which they are reluctant to pass out on personal injury claims."

Each side feeds on the poor image it has of the other. The inevitable result is a vicious circle in which nobody winds up

* The Insurance Information Institute reports that no figures are available on total number of yearly auto claims. But National Safety Council statistics offer a clue: In 1961, 18,500,000 drivers had accidents.

the winner. To assess at this point where the cycle began is futile. Fraudulent claims have probably always plagued the insurance companies to an extent. In recent years the plague has spread fearfully. But when insurance companies dodge payment of legitimate claims, as also happens, they encourage even honest policyholders to do some padding. As padding becomes more prevalent, it increases the companies' tendency toward suspicion, intrusion and reluctance to pay.

One of the main culprits, according to the Claims Bureau, is the ambulance-chasing lawyer whose genius lies in turning a perfectly innocent claim into a swindle. Abetting his efforts on behalf of dishonesty are many tow-truck operators, ambulance and hospital attendants, hospital records-room attendants, individual policemen, nurses and interns who violate confidentiality by steering him to new accident cases. Sometimes these steerers are astonishingly well paid for their work. The Miami *News,* in 1962, running an angry series on fraudulent claimants in Dade County, Florida, stated, "It is common knowledge among lawyers that one of their number built up his large practice by paying policemen $100 for every accident case brought to him."

The crooked attorney often works hand-in-rubber-glove with a like-minded physician. The doctor's specialty, obviously, is to boost a relatively minor accident case into a catastrophe. On the other hand, many a perfectly honest and respectable doctor is also guilty of exaggerating his patients' injuries when an insurance company is involved. Not for personal gain, but out of a sincere belief that the patients would not otherwise get the claims money coming to them. In 1961 prominent Chicago attorney James A. Dooley, in a speech to the insurance section of the American Bar Association, told the lawyers, "Many reputable doctors who have but an occasional encounter with an insurance case regard companies as materialistic monsters interested in paying as little as possible and devoid of common morals."

Mr. Dooley, whose remarks were carried by the *National Underwriter,* went on to point out the excess of zeal displayed by numerous doctors who examine patients on behalf of the insurance companies themselves. These doctors, he said, believe it their duty to *minimize* the extent of the claimants' injuries. Or, if they do not officially minimize, they resort to supplemental (and strictly confidential) memos in which they tell their companies, in effect, "Don't believe a thing I said in the official report."

A somewhat analogous situation exists in regard to automobile claims. A gigantic number of drivers are willing to let cooperative garages hike up the true cost of the repairs by $50 or $100, so that the insurance company is forced to absorb the deductible amount of the policy. The insurance companies have countered by insisting that owners of damaged cars use appraisers and garages designated by the companies. Owners have howled about the shoddy workmanship. In 1963 the Justice Department obtained consent decrees from three insurance trade associations that agreed, on behalf of their member companies, to eliminate the practice.

Most routine insurance claims are handled by claims adjusters whose investigations are relatively superficial. The heaviest investigative guns are trained on claimants in accident cases—especially those in which the injured party alleges impairment or disability. When a preliminary investigation suggests the possibility of fraud, some companies call in a private detective agency to follow through on the investigation.

A private detective working for the oldest and second-largest of the nation's gumshoe agencies—Pinkerton's—told me how he and another detective handled a typical case of this kind. The claimant was a former saleswoman who alleged severe back pains as a result of an automobile accident. She had quit her job, claiming she could no longer stand on her feet all day, and asked for a whopping sum. The case was headed for the courts.

The sleuths staked out near the woman's house—a one-family dwelling occupied by herself and her husband—keeping the front door and driveway in view at all times. For two days nothing happened. The claimant's sole outside activity consisted of retrieving the mail from the mailbox. On the fourth day the claimant drove to a supermarket and loaded up with the week's groceries. Trailing her, the detectives got some good shots as she lifted a heavy box of groceries from a shopping cart and deposited it easily in the trunk of her car. The movies were shown to the claimant's attorney. That case never did reach the courts. However, the private detective who told me this story conceded that on a number of other insurance cases things did not work out so well. Though he took clandestine films, they were inconclusive. The claims might have been genuine.

Secret movie-taking is a favorite way of exposing fraudulent disability claims. Films, after all, cannot be refuted. But other investigative techniques are also used. For instance, sometimes neighborhood checks are made to verify claimants' injuries or illnesses. They have to be done circumspectly, though, for a neighbor might tip off the claimant. On substantial claims the claimant may be shadowed from morning until night in hopes that he will somehow reveal his claim to be spurious.

Occasionally, entrapment is used. One private detective has described how he induced a "blinded" accident victim to read in dim light and how his assistant got another accident victim drunk, then sparred with him outside the bar while the detective filmed the sequence. The latter man was supposed to be suffering from "crippling" leg and back injuries.

Sometimes bribery is resorted to in obtaining documents that might help the insurance company contest a claim. An investigator who has worked on numerous insurance cases told me he was "friendly" with records-room clerks in several big hospitals in his city. These clerks provided him with medical information on claimants who refused to authorize release of such information. In 1955 the former manager of a New York branch of the Social Security Administration was indicted for selling Social Security data, including amounts and sources of income. The buyer, according to the Government, was a private detective agency—which supplied the data to insurance and steamship companies defending personal injury claims.

One of the most controversial of investigative techniques is electronic eavesdropping. The insurance companies and trade associations I contacted vociferously denied that the practice of tapping telephone lines or planting hidden microphones occurs in the insurance field. N. Morgan Woods said, "I haven't heard of a single case." Nevertheless, it may be safely assumed that electronic eavesdropping is at least occasionally resorted to—by a private detective, if not by the insurance company directly. As Professor Harold Lasswell noted in *Conflict of Loyalties,* "In the investigation of insurance claims, for example, this is one of the quickest ways of discovering whether injuries have been grossly exaggerated." Indeed, a lawsuit taking place in Georgia some years ago stemmed from the use of a listening device in the investigation of a personal injury claim. The claimant spent 26 days in a hospital alleging injuries from broken glass in a soft drink. The bottler planted a listening device in her hospital room and discovered the claim to be completely fraudulent. Whereupon she sued for invasion of privacy—and lost.

Just how far can an insurance company—or the sleuthing agency working on its behalf—legally go in the investigation

40

of a claim? Is it free to pull out all the stops, leaving the claimant helpless in the face of whatever intrusion the company deems necessary?

A reasonable assumption would be that the company (or its investigative agency) has a right to conduct as thorough an investigation as the case requires—provided the sleuthing is kept within legal bounds. And so the courts have decreed. It is legal to make neighborhood checks. It is legal to trail a claimant as he goes about his activities. It is legal to take clandestine movies of his movements. Many claimants may have been shocked to discover that they were or had been under surveillance. But few were like the Georgia woman—so aggrieved as to take their complaint to court in the form of an invasion-of-privacy suit, and fewer still have fared any better than she did. As the following case suggests, the investigation must far exceed the bounds of propriety before the courts will act—and even then they might not do so directly.

This case occurred in Louisiana a few years ago and concerned an automobile worker who was injured on the job. The plant's insurance company denied the claim and hired a private detective agency to seek evidence of fraud. The agency performed its task with an excess of zeal, or so the claimant's petition to the Louisiana court suggests:

That these two detectives continued to observe, watch, trail, shadow, eavesdrop, and peek at petitioners during May and June 1955; that these two detectives acting within the scope of their authority and employment in all of their activities constantly shadowed, watched and eavesdropped on petitioners, using binoculars on some occasions; that they took pictures of them without their permission or authority; that they trespassed upon petitioners' property without their consent or permission; that they watched them in their home by peeking through their windows and otherwise harassing and otherwise invading the privacy of petitioners.

A lower court dismissed the action. The plaintiff, refusing to give up, appealed. A higher court conceded the insurance company's right to investigate—but held that the detectives might have violated a "Peeping Tom" statute in peeking through the window. If that was the case, the court reasoned, and the agency was open to criminal prosecution, then a suit in civil damages would also be present. The

41

higher court therefore reversed the original decision and remanded the case to the lower court. At best, then, this was a backhanded acknowledgment of the claimant's right to privacy.

Significantly, one of the few privacy suits won by an individual in an insurance case involved not excessive investigation but unauthorized publication. This case, too, took place in Louisiana. The plaintiff, a Mr. Hamilton, had been involved in an automobile accident in the New Orleans area. He was hospitalized with serious injuries and in no condition to be interviewed about the accident. This put his insurance company in a tight spot. The company needed information about the accident as quickly as possible. Thus it hit upon the scheme that landed it in court. It placed an ad in a New Orleans newspaper *under Mr. Hamilton's name,* though without his knowledge. The ad requested all witnesses to the accident to contact Mr. Hamilton—but underneath his name gave the address and phone number of one of the insurance company's female employees. When the number was dialed, this employee claimed to be Mrs. Hamilton.

Discussing this case in his book, William Zelermyer observes, "Some courts might say that the defendant was justified in choosing this method for the protection of its interests, that such was life, and that ordinary persons could take it. But the Louisiana court was sympathetic." Sympathetic enough to award Mr. Hamilton $5,000 for physical pain, suffering and mental anguish; $2,500 for embarrassment and humiliation; and $5,000 for invasion of his privacy.

The most interesting aspect of this case is the way the insurance company defended its actions. It explained to the court that if the ad had been run over its own name there might not have been as much response—because of the general antagonism against insurance companies! This admission, in open court, delineates with painful clarity the current status between insurers and insureds. This deeply rooted distrust between the public and one of its service institutions may be without precedence and the responsibility for it rests with both sides. As long as its exists, however, you can be certain of one thing: your insurance policy is paid for not only with your cash but with your privacy.

Intrusion

at

Work

4. The Hired Hand . . .
and the Hand That Hires

THERE WAS A time—right up to the approaches of World War II—when a person applying for a job in an office or factory was usually asked to fill out just four items of a personal nature on the employment application form—name, address, Social Security number, and the name of a party to be notified in case of emergency. Well, as Russ White, genial security consultant for the General Electric Company, observes, "Things have changed since then."

Mr. White's observation is low-key. There has been less of a change than a revolution in hiring methods. In the old days the job applicant faced a personnel director who was a keen judge of character and unafraid to play his hunches— bringing to the company a few offbeat types, perhaps, but also adding a lot of fuel to its vitality and creativity. These days the job applicant may face "in-depth" employment application forms, private detectives, lie detector tests, psychological tests, maybe even a direct interview with the company psychologist, before the hiring decision is made. Singly or in combination, these techniques form the methodological approach to hiring—as bloodless as a run through the IBM machine. Safer, too. The techniques make the decision—and take the responsibility.

Nowadays a growing number of employers—the larger corporations particularly—want to know more about the job applicant than he may remember about himself. In a handbook for prospective managers, *Getting and Holding Your Executive Position*, Leon D. Eldot notes: "Questions are becoming more personal in interviews. The executive should orient his thinking to their existence. There is no point in being angry or churlish." What holds true for the executive is equally applicable to white- and blue-collar workers. In the mid-1960's a job applicant in industry, regardless at what level of employment, is likely to be faced with an application blank one to six pages long, eliciting his life history in miniature. He is required to list every place he lived, worked, went to school, with great detail as to dates; his physical characteristics; the nature and duration of all illnesses and accidents; Selective Service information; the relationship to him—and ages of—all his dependents; parents' names; father's occupation and employer; spouse's occupation and employer; and arrest record. If he is an executive he is often required to list the value of his house, amount of mortgage or rent, and to reveal whether he owns his furniture. There is, as Mr. Eldot noted, no point in being churlish—not if you want the job.

Some firms use a double-barreled application form, though the unsuspecting job applicant, trying to recall all the names, places and dates, is unaware of it. That same form he is so feverishly filling out is a *disguised test* for comprehension, ability to organize thoughts, and similar attributes. And so it might be well to pass along another of Mr. Eldot's suggestions as being apt not only for executives but for all prospective employees: "A good plan is to purchase several copies of application forms and test how long it takes to complete the job. The executive will be surprised how much time is consumed without regard to thinking out which answer is going to reflect the greatest credit on himself. It is a big job for a big man and will take a lot of practice to be perfect." Incidentally, making false statements on the application blank is out. Not only is the employee subject to immediate dismissal, he has also committed a crime under the laws of several states, notably New York.

In point of fact it would probably do the job applicant little good to lie because in the 1960's there is an excellent chance that everything he puts down will be verified and amplified by the firm's own security department or by an outside investigative agency. Credit bureaus, private detective agencies and insurance inspection bureaus all do this kind of work. Frederick D. King, vice-president of the

Hooper-Holmes Bureau, whose firm makes personnel checks for such companies as United Aircraft, General Electric, Royal McBee and IBM, says, "This is the most rapidly growing phase of our work." The Burns International Detective Agency, an investigative supermarket whose far-flung operations bring in $30,000,000 worth of business annually, actually has its name on the job application blanks of the firms it services. Such blunt notice to prospective employees has a double psychological value. It discourages falsification and keeps applicants whose background wouldn't stand up under scrutiny from even applying for the job.

Why does a company maintain staff investigators or use outside investigative agencies—both expensive propositions—to check on new employees? Why a full-scale screening when verification of the applicant's statements can be made via phone or mail? An increasing number of firms say that such verification is not enough; few employers, for example, will be completely honest about someone who has left the company's employ without the stimulus of a face-to-face interview. Four principal reasons are usually cited for making personnel checks that, as will be seen, encompass far more than merely substantiating what the applicant has revealed about himself: 1) employee pilferage and theft of trade secrets are becoming fierce problems; 2) training workers is becoming increasingly costly, which means money down the drain if the employee does not work out; 3) union contracts often make it difficult to fire a man even if he turns out to be clearly unacceptable on the job; 4) for defense industries it is a necessity—and for other companies an obligation—to hire only workers whose loyalty to the U.S. can be assured.

The theft problem in business and industry *is* real and ghastly (see Chapter 8). It justifies stringent examination of the prospective employee's job history and any suspicious gaps in employment. Nor is it difficult to get his criminal record, if any: most private detective agencies and security directors have police contacts who provide them with the information. Poor work habits, absenteeism, on-the-job drinking or gambling, and related personality problems are elicited from former employers or supervisors. Educational institutions verify the applicant's schooling. Tests measuring intelligence or dexterity in the job applied for often help to determine the prospective employee's suitability.

Enough? Unfortunately for the state of the job applicant's privacy, far from it. Any outside investigation these days includes a neighborhood check. What the neighbors say about his habits, morals, financial responsibility, and general standing in the community becomes a factor in the hiring decision and finds a home in the applicant's personnel file.

The security manager of a Long Island, New York, factory explained the reason he runs a neighborhood check—and investigates former places of residence—on everyone who comes to work in his organization. It is worth looking at closely. "We can't afford to take chances on hiring somebody who could embarrass us—not in a small community like this," he said. "What an employee does—what he is—reflects on the company. You'd be surprised."

This attitude is present in all paternalistic organizations, whether in small communities or big cities. Overtly it is an expression of concern for the company's public image which, we are led to believe, can be so easily tarnished despite the year-round ministrations of public relations people and ad agencies. But the implication is broader than that. No longer can the employee say, "What I do off the job, how I live my life away from work, is nobody's business but my own." What he does and how he lives becomes the company's business, which implies that it has a right not only to his talents and integrity but to his very personality as well. Thus the company assumes a role much like that of the authoritarian parent who cannot let go of a child long since turned adult. And like that child, the job applicant had better conform.

A personnel manager mentioned alcoholism and homosexuality as traits that would be embarrassing to his firm, while a security director stressed that his organization, despite the intensity with which it investigates applicants for all job categories, just wants to be sure it is getting "normal people." But Professor Louis M. Hacker of Columbia University, who is concerned about the growing tendency of employers to query high school or college teachers about the job applicant's political outlook while in school, says, "When employers talk about normality—about wanting normal people— they are really talking about conformity." He adds that there is a contradiction in this. Employers hunt for people with brains and creativity. At the same time employers don't want anybody who has deviated from the normative standards of society. Yet the very people who have brains and creativity are the ones prone to deviate and experiment.

The philosophy that an employee's personality is for hire becomes even more apparent when companies insist on putting all their prospective employees through lie detector or projective (disguised) psychological tests designed to split an individual's psyche wide open for the appraisal. Not long ago an acquaintance of mine, trying out for a low-level managerial position at one of the major detergent companies, was forced to go through a two-day battery of psychological tests. He left blank a number of impertinent questions—including the one asking how many times a week he had sexual relations with his wife. Nevertheless, he got the job. He might not, however, had he provided an answer displeasing to the psychologist.

In his scathing analysis of the psychological testing industry, *The Brain Watchers*, Martin L. Gross relates the astonishing tale of a twenty-four-year-old married man—an ex-laborer, ex-assembly line worker, ex-Navy petty officer—who applied for a milk routeman's job and was required to take several projective tests. If the requirement was incredible, the results were even more so. The would-be milk routeman was found to be a "meek, submissive, mousy fellow defeated at twenty-four—henpecked with a wife who probably tells him what to do." He didn't get the job. Mr. Gross makes the telling point that "the testing blight" results in "the disintegration of human values in the relationship between employer and employee, between supervisor and those he supervises." Human values are also destroyed when the sleuthing goes too far.

Actually, most negative data encountered in checking on new employees falls outside the personal sphere, if a study recently conducted by an aerospace plant in New York is any indication. (The security director conducting the study declined to be identified since he will publish his own expanded account of it as a trade study.) The study broke down all derogatory reports in the company's files as to job classification and reasons. One out of every 12 reports on shop and office applicants was derogatory, compared to 1 in 4 for executive and fiduciary applicants. The main derogatory aspect in both classifications was unsatisfactory performance on a previous job. But there the similarity ended. For shop and office workers the second main reason for derogatory reports was a criminal record; for executive and fiduciary applicants it was misstatements regarding salary earned in previous jobs.

Background investigations first gained impetus in World War II, as defense plants swung into action and the nation concerned itself with the danger of sabotage. But it was the Cold War emphasis on internal security—and the Government's seemingly endless spawn of loyalty-security investigative programs—that really fired the business community's concern for its own internal security and how best to protect it. (Suspicion being contagious, labor unions and the man on the street followed suit—still further increasing the demand for private "intelligence.") Like kerosene upon the flames was the least-known and possibly the most ill-advised of all the investigative programs—the sweeping Industrial Security Program covering defense contractors and their millions of employees.

The Government is responsible for investigating and clearing defense workers who need access to information labeled TOP SECRET, SECRET and Q. If loyalty-security determinations must be made in industry, and not all authorities are in complete agreement about that, the Government is obviously in the best and fairest position to make them. Yet in the strange workings of the Industrial Security Program, the defense contractors themselves are responsible for granting Confidential clearances to their employees. This remarkable power is subject only to two provisos: 1) the employee must be a U.S. citizen; 2) giving him access to Confidential information would not be inconsistent with the interests of national security.* The Commission on Government Security has estimated that about 59 percent of all clearances issued are of the Confidential category. By 1955 over 2,000,000 employees and managers (out of 3,000,000 covered by the entire program) held Confidential clearances. In short, in the most substantive part of the program private citizens have been given the responsibility of scrutinizing other private citizens and judging their loyalty. The Defense Department, under whose aegis Confidential clearances are issued, maintains that it has neither the time nor the manpower to handle an investigative-administrative program of such magnitude.

The situation has invited the creation of an investigative hodge-podge. It is fraught with possibilities for the rankest invasions of the job applicant's political privacy. Both have occurred in full measure.

Some companies have proceeded reluctantly under the Industrial Security Program, either doing no investigating or, more often, banking on the commercial investigative agencies, many of which are not equipped to make security checks. Other companies, spurred on by their security obligations, have built up elaborate investigative staffs and dos-

---

* If the employee admits, on his clearance application form, to having been a member of a Communist-front organization or to having relatives in the Sino-Soviet bloc countries, the government makes the security determination.

siers, expanding their activities to cover not only employees working in classified areas but everyone in the plant. Thus, the security chief for Temco Electronics Division of Ling-Temco-Vought, Inc., has said, "Regardless of where a man is going to work, his background should be looked at as carefully as if he were going to work on classified material." "Specialists" on subversive activities, blacklists in hand, have lent their facilities to the private loyalty program. Plants totally uninvolved in defense work have caught the fever and adopted their own unofficial loyalty-testing program. They have done so out of conviction, for better public relations, or —in some cases—because of the activity of pressure groups. For instance, a man applying for a job in a company making dairy products was surprised to find that the firm investigated him for possible subversion before he was taken on.

Inevitably, security checks themselves have become a profitable activity. Perhaps this is the reason there seems to be a lot of backbiting in the field. I have heard plant security officers (former FBI agents) decry the shoddy work performed by private detectives. I have heard private detectives insist that security officers are often overrated. One can only speculate at the varying levels of competence exercised in this field which ferrets out an individual's most private thoughts and actions to assay his loyalty.

Far from being happy with the role of formal inquisitor that has been thrust upon it, industry is most uneasy about its clearance-granting responsibilities. Making unofficial loyalty checks on its own behalf is one thing; making them officially is another. If a company errs and is found to harbor security risks it faces bad publicity, possibly a Congressional investigation, and perhaps a delay in receiving its next government contract. Yet it is supposed to make the loyalty determination without having access to government records. Though Ralph S. Brown, Jr., suggests in *Loyalty and Security* that a few of the bigger defense contractors may have some information trickle in from local FBI agents, it is safe to assume that most companies do without. Thus it is not surprising that industry's attitude toward the whole situation is a negative one; as Timothy J. Walsh, 1st vice-president of the American Society for Industrial Security, states, "The burden of security investigations should be left to the Government. Access to government information should be government business."

Labor unions say that with employers granting clearances, the union-oriented job applicant is in an extremely vulnerable position. Thomas E. Harris, Associate General Counsel for the AFL-CIO, enlarged upon this attitude in a statement prepared for the Senate Subcommittee on Constitutional Rights, which in 1959 studied methods for providing due process of law in federal loyalty-security programs. Harris noted that "it is the easiest thing in the world for an employer on the basis of data furnished by some private source to deny employment to applicants known to be militant union adherents. These applicants will, of course, not be told that they are being rejected because they are union men, or that they are being rejected for any security reason. They simply will not be hired." He went on to state that the government program encourages unofficial loyalty checks and allows management to pretend it is being motivated by patriotism.

In any event, the present situation is patently unfair to the job applicant. He has no recourse if, for any reason, he is deemed a security risk. He has no way to defend himself against mistaken identity, unfounded gossip, or false and malicious accusations. He has no opportunity for a hearing or review, as do employees already on the job. If the firm does not choose to tell him why he was turned down—and most of the time, to avoid complications, it won't—he may never know that he has been designated a security risk by someone somewhere. According to the regulations, an employer is not empowered to *deny* clearances (only the Government may do that). In practice, he has that power by simply not taking on the controversial applicant.

The Defense Department's 21 criteria on the makeup of security risks include such items as drug addiction, excessive use of intoxicants, sexual perversion and criminal conduct. By far the greater part of the list, and the most troublesome because of its loose wording, relates to disloyalty.

Some private loyalty-security investigators—*The Reporter* has dubbed them "commercial Commie catchers"—performed similar functions for the FBI or a military intelligence agency and have vast experience in this field. Many more are shiny-eyed young men who sally forth from their investigative agencies armed with the worthy ambition to "catch a Commie," but sadly equipped for a task upon whose result rests a person's job and, at times, reputation. The private eyes no more than the contractors themselves have access to government files. (A few occasionally boast of FBI connections but this is usually window-dressing for potential clients.) For the most part, the investigators have no special training that would enable them to distinguish between nonconformists, people with a highly developed social consciousness, and actual subversives. (FBI agents at least receive indoctrination courses in civil liberties.) As a candid spokesman for the Retail Credit Co. says, "We recognize that our security investigation is a preliminary step and is by no means the exhaustive and intensive study generally associated with a 'security check.' "

What kinds of questions does the investigator ask the applicant's neighbors, former employers, teachers and/or associates to elicit information about his loyalty? He may ask about the applicant's reading matter, his political opinions, his churchgoing habits, his possible participation in "peace" movements, freedom rides or mixed white-and-Negro parties. He may ask whether the applicant has signed petitions, handed out literature for any cause, expressed preference for a foreign country, been in the habit of criticizing the U.S. He may ask if the applicant has seemed unduly sympathetic to the country of his birth (if foreign-born). He may simply ask if the applicant is considered to be a loyal American. His questions may be sensible or they may be grounded in personal prejudice.

(If the job applicant is interviewed directly, as he might be by a plant security officer, the problem of his loyalty could be approached obliquely. The security manager for a West Coast missile plant, writing in *Industrial Security,* a slick journal published by the American Society for Industrial Security, revealed to his colleagues that he uses the Bible as a "secret weapon." Explaining that atheists, Communists or fellow travelers would take exception to the Bible and its teachings, he advised, "If you find yourself somewhat in doubt concerning a person's political views or affiliations, you'll find a discussion on some scripture or lesson from the Bible quite enlightening.")

In an effort to inject greater regard for constitutional rights in the federal loyalty-security programs, the Defense Department in 1962 issued a memorandum cautioning government security investigators and security review boards that "the probing of a person's thoughts or beliefs and questions about his conduct, which have no security implications, are unwarranted," and offered 26 kinds of queries deemed improper or irrelevant. The private investigator is bound by no such guidelines. Though one would wish the story to be apocryphal, among the investigators I interviewed is one who insists

51

that some of his colleagues approach security investigations from the viewpoint of the subject's religion, as follows:

"Jews, suspect; Unitarians, suspect; 'watch out' for Methodists; Congregationalists, 'maybe yes, maybe no'; Presbyterians, 'be careful'; Baptists, 'it all depends; take a look at the minister and where the church is located'; Catholics, not suspect."

A much more likely hazard for the job applicant, particularly if he has involved himself in activities disapproved of by his neighbors, is to be the target of unfounded accusations not properly checked by the investigator. Private detectives who have questioned informants closely to determine why particular job applicants were being called "pro-Communist" often heard explanations like the following: "He's critical of big business"; "he reads *The Nation* and believes in unilateral disarmament"; "he's all hot for the U.N." Possibly the wildest case of all involved the job applicant who was accused of being a Communist—because he was a practicing nudist!

The tendency of some private investigators to accept accusations without closely questioning the source or checking with other informants is reflected in their reports. A proper investigative report identifies the informants and gives specific reasons for the accusations, enabling the security or personnel manager to evaluate the data. But it is not unusual for reports to say something vague and utterly damaging, as, "There is no evidence to prove that he is a Communist, but there is good reason to believe that he has pro-Communist sympathies," without spelling out those reasons. In 1955 *The Reporter*, in an article titled "The Private Eyes," pointed out that private loyalty investigators tend to set their standards for clearance even higher than those adopted by the Government. The reason is to anticipate and prevent any future finding of subversion by federal or Congressional agencies. The specter of the late Senator Joseph McCarthy, who charged that Communists were active in such firms as Westinghouse, Allis-Chalmers and Bethlehem Steel, is still present. Thus in some cases the vaguest suggestion of pro-Communist tendencies, even if unsubstantiated, becomes the basis for a derogatory report.

The article in *The Reporter* told of a Dun & Bradstreet personnel security report marked "Unfavorable" though the report "noted only that three sources claimed the applicant had expressed ideas of a 'definite subversive tendency,' had possessed 'a subversive turn of mind,' and had distributed 'pamphlets and leaflets . . . of a subversive nature.' There the investigator's report ended, without any attempt to define what the three sources, who were controverted by other references, meant by the word 'subversive.' "

When I tried to find out how Dun & Bradstreet personnel security reports are handled these days, the company was reluctant to discuss the matter. After I attempted for several weeks to interview some D & B official on the subject, a representative admitted, "Nobody here likes to stick his neck out on that."

What is the reaction of the security director who receives a vaguely worded report? We may assume that the job applicant not possessed of some hard-to-find skill stands little chance of being hired. The security director is not sinister; merely doing the best he can in a tough role in which he is called upon to be a master juggler. He must please the Government's security agencies by living up to their directives, advance his company's cause (and his own career), avoid antagonizing the other departments within his plant, secure the cooperation of all the firm's employees, and (theoretically) play fair with the job applicant. Clearly, if he cannot keep all the balls in the air, the job seeker is going to be the first to fall. Why take a chance—especially with a big labor pool to choose from?

He may also be reflecting his company's policy to take on no one about whom there is the slightest suspicion. The controversial Attorney General's list of Communist front organizations provides a case in point. Anybody who was ever a member of one, even if he joined long ago for nonsubversive reasons or before the alleged Communist infiltration took place, has a tough time getting a job in many of the nation's defense plants.

This tendency on the part of defense plants to shy away from hiring anybody who might turn out to be the least bit controversial provides some ironic situations. Two years ago a woman I know—one whose politics are decidedly conservative—applied for a job she was well qualified to handle. While the position didn't call for clearance, it did require her to be bonded. Several days after she filled out her job application form an insurance inspector interviewed her about the bond. She was subsequently turned down for the job. Some time later, out of curiosity, she had a high-placed friend of hers within the firm quietly check out the reason. What was it? While interviewing her the insurance inspector had, according to her file, noticed a "quantity of subversive materials" in her apartment. Upon hearing this, my acquaintance was genuinely nonplused as to what those materials might be. Then she realized that in her bookshelf, gathering dust, was an 8-volume set of Lenin's works someone had given her years before.

The job applicant branded a security risk for whatever reason may be faced with a calamity far greater than the denial of one job. Many employment opportunities may be closed to him in his trade or profession. If the company that turned him down is the dominant one in his community, he might as well pack up and move. Attorney Joseph L. Rauh told the Subcommittee on Constitutional Rights about one security risk who was turned down an incredible 113 times by companies that had advertised in the help-wanted columns for jobs he could fill.

And there is the sorry tale of the female wire inspector who was declared a security risk and given a choice between taking a lower-paying job within her firm or resigning altogether. She chose to resign. Later, at a security hearing, she learned why she had been declared a risk. The charge stemmed from the fact that she had associated—on the job only—with a Communist Party member who worked right behind her. Though the review board agreed to clear the wire inspector if her former employer would send in additional information, the firm never bothered to do so. The result: she was fired from five successive jobs as soon as her employment references were checked.

Just as difficult a time may be had by anyone listed—with or without his knowledge—by the American Security Council, which has compiled over 1,000,000 names of allegedly subversive individuals and organizations. It was inevitable, of course, that a government program making private companies responsible for spotting security risks would eventually give birth to an industrial blacklist. Though the American Security Council has declared itself to be politically nonpartisan, its roots go deep into the far right. Among the many industrial leaders and retired military men involved in the organization is General Robert E. Wood, former head of Sears, Roebuck & Co., who has backed a number of far right groups. ASC field director is W. Cleon Skousen, a former FBI agent and author of a book, *The Naked Communist*. Richard Dudman, in *Men of the Far Right,* reveals Skousen's book to be "a Bible of the right-wing movement and is promoted heavily by many of the extremist groups."

Founded in 1955 by William F. Carroll, another former FBI agent, the ASC provides its subscribers with information on anyone who has shown even the slightest indication of left wing associations. Though the organization is also involved in mapping Cold War strategy and puts out a newsletter, only its screening service will be discussed here. It conducts no field investigations, operating solely as a collector of names. And where do the names come from? The ASC has assembled them from files kept by the late Harry Jung, publisher of an extreme right-wing newspaper, *The American Vigilante;* from the records of several corporations that investigated communist activity within their own plants; from other private security organizations that disbanded; and from Congressional and state antisubversive hearings. Names come from over 6,000 publications clipped each week, from newspapers, books and magazines, from speeches by alleged left-wingers, from the letterheads of groups on the Attorney General's list, and from petitions sponsored or approved by Communist or left-wing organizations.

What kind of standard guides the inclusion of names in the Council's subversive files? John W. Fisher, ASC president, has announced, "Interest for or against the free enterprise system—that's the thing that starts our interest. If the situation is in line with the current Communist Party line, then it becomes of interest to us." This assertion must be viewed in relation to J. Edgar Hoover's comment that "the danger of indiscriminately alleging that someone is a Communist merely because his views on a particular subject happen to parallel the official party position is obvious." The ASC net, it seems, is broad indeed. As the New York *Post* has observed, "Thus a man (without his knowing it) may wind up in the American Security Council files simply because he has, for example, come out against H-Bomb tests. The Communist Party line also is against H-Bomb tests. The Council does not say that all H-Bomb test opponents are Communists, but the implication is there when a prospective employer gets the dossier on an applicant."

The Council has grown with startling rapidity. Early in 1960 it had 450 members. In 1963 membership exceeded 3,200. Subscribers include such substantial firms as General Electric, Allstate Insurance Co., Illinois Central Railroad, Stewart-Warner Corp., Motorola, Inc., and Sears, Roebuck & Co. With some 24,000 industrial facilities involved in defense work, the organization can be expected to keep on expanding as rapidly in the future. John M. Fisher is a member of the American Society for Industrial Security, to which most of industry's top security officials belong.

There is an irony attached to the frenzied activity in the area of private loyalty checks, with its creepy peering-over-everybody's-shoulder aspects, its probing of personal beliefs, its tendency (as with any such program) to create an atmosphere of fear that suppresses dissent of any kind and stifles individual thought. The irony is this: while the Defense Department apparently hangs on to the Confidential classification for dear life, many other interested and authoritative parties are convinced it simply is not essential to the nation's security.

For example, the Commission on Government Security, a body organized by the Government itself expressly for the purpose of suggesting changes in the loyalty-security programs, stated in 1957: "The fact that the Government now permits private industry to clear employees for access to confidential information and materials, without requiring a security check of any sort and merely on the basis of a statement of citizenship, indicates that the degree of risk to the national security is not substantial." And Timothy Walsh, urging a governmental reevaluation of the Confidential category, says, "The vast amount of material should be critically reexamined and eliminated from classification wherever possible—to the extent that the classification itself be eliminated."

None of the foregoing is to deny that there have been Communist attempts to infiltrate defense plants. Only the most naïve could deny that there are subversive elements among us. A drastically curtailed loyalty-security program covering employees in highly sensitive industrial jobs is probably unavoidable so long as present world tensions continue. But the way to internal security is not reached by indiscriminately seeding the countryside with insecurity. Loyalty investigations and determinations are the business of the U.S. Government, which has the know-how and the facilities—and over whose activities the citizen has at least some control. Professor Andrew Hacker of Cornell University has pointed out that "the only responsibility of corporations is to make profits, thus contributing to a prosperous economic system." That would seem to be a far more worthy function than for them to be called upon—or take the initiative—in maintaining a vigilante system.

To be sure, relieving industry of the burden of making security checks would not end the unofficial program. Its momentum is, in any case, too strong to stop at once. Many firms would continue to make preliminary loyalty determinations and turn down job applicants whose report is labeled UNFAVORABLE. The professional name collectors would still continue to collect them. But to some degree, and with continuing reform at government level, the present abuses would be lessened. And the Government would no longer sanction the proposition that private citizens have the ability or the right to peer indiscriminately into other private citizens' lives to decide whether they are loyal enough to get a job.

5. The Executive File

DEFENSE WORKERS ARE scrutinized carefully but the blockbuster investigations, the ones that often dig up every detail in a man's life from the hour he was born to the day of the probe, are reserved for executives. No item of information is left uncovered if it has some relevance to his character, personality, education and ability. I have seen executive reports that were 25 typewritten single-spaced pages long, and they run longer. Such reports are not only meant to uncover any derogatory information that might give the hiring company pause before signing the executive to a $25,000-a-year job. Frequently they also tell whether he would fit into the closely knit corporate community. Judging by the dossiers, William H. Whyte, Jr.'s, Organization Man is still very much sought.

A few investigative agencies specialize in reporting on executives and individuals whose jobs call for a high degree of fiduciary responsibility. One such is Bishop's Service, a long-established organization located, appropriately enough, in the Wall Street area. William Chiarello, the agency's dynamic president, alluded to the scope of the executive probe when he explained, "As a result of our investigation, a portrait of the whole man emerges. Not only is there a continuity of events in the subject's life from birth to the present, the report also offers a projection of future possibilities." He added, however, that only the bare—and sometimes sensational—facts are presented. The agency does not evaluate them.

What is an executive report like? How is the investigation carried out? Chiarello outlined how his investigators handled a typical case. This one involved a fifty-year-old mechanical engineer being considered for a job that would afford him a considerable increase in earnings. Call the man Eric. The prospective employer wanted to know if Eric would be right for the job and justify the much higher salary.

The investigator assigned to the case looked first into Eric's finances. What was his credit rating? Had he acquired any sizable debts? What did his bankers think of him? Public records were combed for bankruptcy proceedings and for litigation. Law enforcement officers indicated whether he had a police record. Subversive lists were checked. Property records were examined to determine the value of the house in which he lived and the mortgages thereon. (Thus it does no good for an executive to misstate the facts on his resumé or job application form; he will be found out.)

Eric's scholastic background was thoroughly gone into. Did he actually go to the schools and receive the degrees he had listed? Professors were interviewed to fleshen out the academic portion of his portrait. What kind of a student had he been? In the top third? Brilliant, average, mediocre? What was his behavior—disciplined or unruly? Had any honors come his way? What about extracurricular activities, and what about his imagination and creativity?

His work history was scrutinized minutely. Why did he leave his former jobs? Was he fired? Did he resign? Was he forced to resign? What about his stature in the field, his achievements and integrity? Would he be eligible for re-employment? Did he get along with superiors and subordinates? Did he give credit where it was due, or credit himself with work actually done by his subordinates?

People who had known Eric for years were questioned in depth, often under a suitable pretext so he would not know that his future employer was checking on him. What were Eric's areas of strength and weakness? How mature was he? Did he have the ability to make his own decisions and stick by them? If so, did that mean he was stubborn? What about his initiative and judgment? Would you give him a large sum of money and let him handle a business by himself?

The investigator concluded the inquiry by delving into Eric's social life. Was there anything derogatory about his character and reputation? Did he drink to excess? Any scandalous situations, such as excessive gambling or a woman problem? Was there anything in his background that might be used by unscrupulous parties to put pressure on him? What about his mode of living? Any question about his associates? To what clubs and professional associations does he belong? (Not mentioned by Chiarello, but listed in executive reports I have seen, is mention of the executive applicant's religious activities, if any. If he is a regular churchgoer or otherwise active in his religion the point is stressed as indicating his favorable character. Of course, it also advises the corporation just what his religion is. Detectives working in states that have antidiscrimination statutes do not seem to be hamstrung by the limitation. A private detective in New York, which has such a statute, told me with a grin that people "volunteer" the information and he puts it into the reports because his clients want it.)

To finish up with Eric, however, it is extremely unlikely that he ever got the job. He had trouble handling people and there had been some question, on a former job, about his ability to handle tricky situations. He had also padded his scholastic background. About 20 percent of the executive checks made by Bishop's Service turn up unfavorable information.

Up to a point, a good case can be made for the necessity of invading the executive's privacy. Chiarello offered the following reasons for the growing popularity of executive reports:

Expenses. It often takes as long as six months (sometimes much longer) for a firm to find out if the executive it has hired is satisfactory. By that time he has cost the company roughly three times his salary.

Fringe benefits. Thirty years ago the inept executive was fired—and forgotten. Today things are not that simple. Termination may present the company with sticky problems it will have to solve before getting rid of the man, problems having to do with fringe benefits like stock options and pension plans. There may also be a labor contract involved. Says Chiarello, "Benefits lock an executive into the company—and lock the company into him."

Specialization. The average vice-president today has under his jurisdiction not only foremen and lower-echelon people, but also other executives who are themselves in charge of specific departments. Such executives, especially if highly skilled, are tempting prey for raiders from other companies. The vice-president has to know how to handle situations like that. If he is inept he may not only do a poor job in his own bailiwick but also cause the firm to lose some really good men.

Phonies. There has been a marked increase, in recent years, in con artists who apply for high-salaried, top-level positions. Such men are smooth talkers and know their way around, but are totally unqualified for the job. Their talent lies in bluffing. They know that sooner or later their masquerade will be exposed, and that is precisely their game. They play for time. Even if the company catches up with him after a year or so, the con man will still be as much as $30,000 or $40,000 plus expenses ahead.

In one case a gifted and nervy phony—Mr. Sharpie might be a good pseudonym for him—answered an ad calling for a high-salaried electrical engineer. Seemingly well educated, persuasive, he talked a good game of electrical engineering and had an imposing background. He appeared to be just the man for the job. The president of the firm interviewed him three times, then hired him. After a six-month indoctrination period, Mr. Sharpie was promoted and given a handsome three-year contract. Shortly thereafter, the other engineers in his department stalked into the president's office and handed the astonished official an ultimatum. Charging Mr. Sharpie with gross incompetence, they insisted that either he be fired or they would quit in a body. He was fired.

However, this turn of events did not faze Mr. Sharpie, for he immediately sued for breach of contract. At this point Bishop's Service was called in to handle a belated investigation. The result: Mr. Sharpie had never gone beyond the second year of high school, did not even have on-the-job training as an electrical engineer, was wanted as a swindler by the police of six states, was a bigamist, and was living with the runaway wife of a banker. Confronted with the details of his rather eventful life, he dropped the lawsuit in a hurry.

It would seem that Mr. Sharpie was, in some respects, sharper than the president of the firm, who had not even done the most rudimentary kind of background checking. But no matter. The point is made. Into every executive applicant's life an investigator must intrude. Given a reasonably competent investigative job, there is nothing the prospective manager can hide. An argumentative personality, a mistress, heavy debts, a compulsion to gamble or drink—all have turned up on executive background reports and cost otherwise able men the jobs they hoped to get.

In a Burns Agency case, the background check uncovered the fact that an exceptionally keen executive applicant was an equally exceptionally heavy drinker. The corporation considering this man read the report, reflected, then came back with a query: "How well does he handle his drinking?" Further investigation disclosed that the subject had remarkable imbibing powers: he could drink five men under the table and walk away in full command of his senses. He was hired.

This does not happen often. More typical is a case recently handled by another detective agency. This one involved a crackerjack salesman whose own organization was about to promote him to a sales manager's position. However, the probe spotlighted his serious drinking problem. It was also learned that he was quite garrulous when drunk. He was passed up for the promotion. He could have been a security risk insofar as confidential pricing data was concerned.

The salesman's story points up the fact that by no means does only the newcomer to the corporate scene (or to the hiring firm) become an investigative target. Even if an employee has been on the payroll for years, and his personnel file is already fat with facts, a new investigation may well be run on him when he is being considered for promotion to executive rank. Knowing him from the on-the-job point of view, even if he has an excellent record, is not enough for the company. It wants the full exposure—secretly, of course. A similar situation applies for executives involved in lengthy indoctrination periods. These are the managers shifted to another department or a different plant every couple of years. Though their superiors write fitness reports on them, many firms prefer to supplement these with an objective outside report. The Burns Agency has noted a decided increase in the demand for reports of this character. (Burns and other detective agencies have also been giving a growing number of lie detector tests to executives. This phenomenon is described in the following chapters.)

Investigative-minded corporations have not only been probing their own applicants and working managers, they have also been invading the privacy of desirable executives who work in another firm. Coveting the executive, intending to make a strong try at plundering him, the corporation puts him surreptitiously under the magnifying glass to be sure he has no personal problems or character failings to mar his handsome business profile. As has been well publicized by Vance Packard and others in recent years, professional executive recruiting agencies do the same. One thing not generally known is what the raiding corporation wants most eagerly to learn—and it is this: will his own company put up a fight or let him go without a fuss? If a fight it would be, the raider becomes really ardent and the intrigue to snatch him begins in earnest. On the other hand, says a detective whose busy schedule never takes him out of the corporate world, if the executive's own firm is unwilling to fight for him, the pirate frequently loses all interest, like the neurotic lover who hungers only for the girls most difficult to get.

As for the executive, he goes about his daily tasks never realizing that the details of his private and business life are being picked through like so much clothing at a rummage sale—and as irreverently, if less noisily. He may learn that somebody has been asking questions about him, but somebody is always asking questions for one reason or other, and it does not register. As Packard has pointed out, the executive often becomes a product, looked over by buyer and seller while he remains passive. The fact that his privacy is being capriciously invaded bothers no one of those involved. After all, what do you do with a product you are not sure of? You peer inside to see if it works.

Some of the professional recruiting firms have their own full-time sleuths; many others call on the more reputable private detective agencies for help in checking on job applicants. The recruiter has to be certain that the executive he is selling is of Grade A quality. If the man he peddles turns out to be third-rate or damaged goods, his reputation suffers— and a firm that receives thousands of dollars for each executive placed can hardly afford to be frivolous with its reputation.

Nevertheless, it seems that not all of the recruiting firms are equally ethical. So has been the experience of one of the most respected private detective agencies in New York City. Declining to be identified by name, an official of the agency explained that sometimes a hiring firm orders a background report from him through the recruiter handling the placement. If derogatory information turns up in the report, the recruiter storms that he will be unable to sell the executive involved and insists on having the negative data removed. Rejecting the inevitable bait of additional business, the agency refuses. Needless to say, no added business is forthcoming from this recruiter, for there are more cooperative detective agencies around.

If a good argument for executive reports can be made in terms of evaluating the manager's abilities, character, education, and so forth, the argument becomes less defensible when the privacy invasions center with unreasonable force on what in more genteel times was known as the "sanctity of the home." And the trend is toward just such invasions. One manifestation of it is the corporations' increasing conviction that the executive applicant's wife is a fit subject for detailed investigation before the hiring decision is made. Chiarello has noticed that more companies are asking more questions about wives. Vance Packard, in *The Pyramid Climbers,* quotes an official of Ward Howell Associates: "With almost any executive job paying over $18,000 the prospective boss wants to meet the wife before he hires the man." Martin L. Gross discovered that psychological testing for executives' wives is on the increase. Even more to the point is the terse comment of a high-level corporation executive quoted in *Business Week:* "We hire the lady, too." The lady is often met, not only in person, but through the pages of a clandestine investigative report.

One sleuth whose job it sometimes is to inspect the distaff side of the executive's family reveals, "My clients want to know what she's like in her present community. They want to know how she'll get along with all the other executives and their wives if her husband is hired. They want to know if she's hubby's little helpmate."

To begin with, he finds out how much stability there is in the marriage. This opens up far more than a casual glance might suggest. Does she nag the man? Mother him? Does she do things to destroy his confidence in himself? Is she more mature than he is, making a comparison between them disadvantageous to him? Does she basically dislike men—revealing her antipathy, perhaps, by continual illnesses or chronic extravagances?

The backyard-gossip quality of some of this information really comes into focus among the other points he checks for, such as, who runs the show in the family? Do the neighbors like her? Is she sociable? Is she too sociable and has a man problem? What are her drinking habits like? Is she outspoken or the quiet type? Does she feel very strongly about any social or political problem? What clubs does she belong to?

Underlying all this snooping are the points the corporation really wants to know: will she fit in? Is she a troublemaker? Is there something about her relationship with the executive applicant that might cause him to fall down on the job?

Even the children are not neglected. A personnel director told me, "If a man can't handle his kids, he may have a problem with subordinates." And one executive report that came to my attention had a paragraph in it that said, "The subject is described as not the permissive-type of parent, who strictly governs the conduct of his girl and two boys. Universally, their behavior is most favorably regarded and they are described with unanimity as very nice and well-behaved children."

Executive screening has not been kept a deep, dark secret; most applicants likely assume they will be investigated—though the extent of the inquiry might surprise the less sophisticated. I have not heard of a single case in which the applicant stormed angrily into his prospective employer's office upon learning that his neighbors and former associates have been questioned about him. The attitude seems to be, "That's the way things are." Just a passive reaction? Perhaps. But younger executives and trainees have their entire adult lives been exposed to the pressures of the Goldfish Age. Privacy has become a lot less meaningful to them. Too, once the investigation is concluded, and they are hired, there may well be a positive feeling about the intrusion: a feeling of security that comes with having "passed" the screening process much as a student passes a college exam. There is the added security of knowing that all their colleagues-to-be have gone through the same trial by fire. As a junior executive put it, "Who wants to work with a lot of oddballs?"

The executive's wife is more apt to react defensively if she learns that private detectives have invaded her privacy, especially if she already bears some resentment toward the corporate world. In one case involving a protesting wife, an untalented private detective was at fault. He had asked too many pointed questions about her sex life. So outraged was the woman, she forced her husband to refuse the job.

Though the executive's investigative file is privileged communication, not to be bandied about like the gossip items in the morning paper (and usually isn't), it is not so privileged that it may not come back to haunt him at a later date. There is always the hazard of a leak—particularly in life-and-death battles for power, when anything can happen. Even an innocent bystander's file may be used as ammunition in the fray.

A detective specializing in corporation work told me of his involvement in an intramural corporate slugfest. The scene was a West Coast manufacturing firm whose president and vice-president were engaged in a bitter tug-of-war. Shortly after the president brought a new middle-echelon executive into the firm, the vice-president ordered an extensive background report on the newcomer, hoping to come up with some dirt. All the investigator could undercover was a minor scandal with a call girl that had taken place 7 years before.

Altogether, the report was favorable—too favorable for the vice-president who had ordered it. He wanted the investigator to rewrite it, slanting the report to present the newcomer in a poor light. His intention was to show the file to the chairman of the board, a man of rigid morality. The chairman, he figured, would conclude that the president had exercised bad judgment in hiring the new executive. At the same time his own status would be enhanced. But the president somehow learned of the scheme. He too approached the private investigator—offering to pay him a handsome sum if he would slant the report to play down the derogatory information! The investigator refused both requests and has no idea what finally happened. All three men are still at their posts. He doubts that the newcomer ever found out to what use the intimate facts of his private life were going to be put.

6. The Lie Detector:

Industry's Electric Chair

Part One

MOST PEOPLE ARE at once fascinated and repelled by the idea of the lie detector, technically known as the polygraph. As one woman who went through a polygraph examination remarked afterwards, "I had the feeling that a machine was peering into my soul." In recent years the polygraph has received widespread publicity regarding some of its soul-peering functions. It evokes an image of criminal suspects being interrogated, applicants for highly sensitive government jobs being screened, potential bank tellers and others who handle large sums of money being checked out.

At one time this image might have been accurate. Now it is just plain out of date. Whatever you do and wherever you work, you may well be strapped to a lie detector someday as a condition of getting a job, keeping it, or clearing yourself in the event of a cash or inventory shortage.

The way the lie detector has been catching on in popularity is little short of amazing. Probably no other phenomenon of our times so aptly illustrates the arrival of the Goldfish Age. Probably no other technique of intrusion will ultimately bring on more of a battle royal between the forces promoting its general acceptance and the forces that consider it a vicious instrument for invading privacy.

Official statistics regarding the extent to which business and industry use lie detection services are as yet unavailable. While many firms are enthusiastic about subjecting their employees to polygraph examinations, few are so far willing to make their enthusiasm publicly known. Significantly enough, official Washington has been just as reticent in granting the polygraph public recognition, though several government agencies have used it for personnel screening. So controversial is the lie detector, in fact, that periodically Congressmen threaten investigations into the government agencies' use of it. This happened again in 1963. And the same year, President John F. Kennedy said "it was a mistake" for the Defense Department to have asked high government officials to clear themselves via the polygraph during an investigation of a news leak. The tests were called off.

Despite the fact that most companies using the polygraph would rather not advertise the fact, we can get some idea of what is going on. There are about 600 polygraph examiners in the U.S. at present (more people are going into the business all the time), and the *Industrial Relations News* indicates that examiners now do 80 percent of their work for private companies, the rest for police departments. The New York office of the Burns Agency has more than doubled the number of lie detector examinations it has given over the past few years. In 1960 *Business Week* told of the Keeler Polygraph Institute and John E. Reid & Associates, two Chicago polygraph firms, that have indicated their volume of business to be 8 to 10 times what it was a decade past. Several years ago only a few hundred Texan firms required their employees to take lie tests as a condition of starting or continuing employment. The number has zoomed to over 5,000 and in 1961 the Fort Worth *Star-Telegram* reported just one detective agency to be giving tests to workers in the Fort Worth-Dallas area at the fantastic rate of 25,000 a year.

What kind of companies request their employees to undergo lie tests? As the figures suggest, there is a great deal of diversity among them. Some of the firms that have made use of the polygraph are McKesson & Robbins, a pharmaceutical manufacturer; First Distributors, a mail order house; Palmer House, a swank Chicago hotel; Children's Bus Service Inc. of New York; Thillens Checkcashers, a check cashing service. Among the companies that insist on giving lie detector tests to everyone who comes on the payroll are department stores, country clubs, liquor stores, hardware stores, vending machine firms, chemical companies, service stations, optical supply houses, trucking firms.

This is, of course, only a fraction of the total range. Leonard Lowell, Chairman of the Board of Dale Systems, and a great polygraph booster, told me: "Every type of retail store and manufacturing outfit now uses polygraph checks, both for pre-employment and when there has been pilferage." He added emphatically, "I have never seen anything as effective as this for picking off undesirables."

Polygraph checks are catching on in nonindustrial fields, too. Several polygraph examiners have told me that husbands and wives involved in domestic squabbles now employ lie tests to prove (or perhaps fail to prove) their fidelity. Insurance companies sometimes use the tests in claims disputes, if the claimant is willing. At times lawyers insist on giving potential clients lie detector tests before accepting the case.

Mr. Lowell relates a revealing incident involving a lawyer. The attorney had been approached by a CPA accused of embezzlement. The CPA insisted on his innocence, but the lawyer was unsure and did not want to represent the man if he was guilty. A lie detector examination was agreed upon. According to the results of the test, the CPA was guilty— though even afterwards he vehemently denied his guilt. The lawyer pulled out of the case, his faith in the polygraph manifestly greater than in his would-be client. Presumably, the CPA found someone else to represent him. We may take it for granted he would not again be rash enough to volunteer taking a polygraph examination.

Aside from the worrisome new uses to which it is being applied, there is really nothing new about the polygraph. The most advanced and expensive lie detector on the market today works on the same principles known to nineteenth-century scientists—namely, that certain physiological changes occur within a person when he tells a lie. The whole thing began with Italian criminologist Cesare Lombroso. In 1895 he announced to the world that he could establish the guilt or innocence of suspected criminals by taking their blood pressure while they were being questioned. Shortly, famed Swiss psychiatrist C. G. Jung made a discovery that fitted in neatly with Lombroso's: he concluded that it was possible to detect attempts at lying or evasion by measuring the changing resistance of the skin to electricity. In the early 1900's another Italian criminologist, Vittorio Benussi, made a study which proved that the breathing rate of subjects under interrogation changed when they attempted deception.

Despite later refinements, these three principles form the basis of most lie detectors. Lie detector? As J. Edgar Hoover, never one to show much fondness for the polygraph, has put it, "The name is a complete misnomer." The "lie detector" detects neither lies nor truths. It simply measures and records the physiological changes that occur in a person when he is undergoing any kind of emotional disturbance—as, say, when he is telling a fib. The interpretation is left entirely to the examiner—making him, not the apparatus, the real lie detector.

Right here one of the major weaknesses—and dangers—of the polygraph comes hovering into view. It can be brought into even sharper focus by observing the apparatus at work, the examiner on the job, the subject in the interrogation chair.

What happens to that subject? What would happen to you if you were required to take a polygraph examination—as well might be the case one day?

The examiner, a relaxed young man, will greet you affably as you come into his office at the appointed hour. A moment's exchange of pleasantries and he will lead you into the interrogation room. This is usually of medium size, somewhere around 15′ x 15′, with acoustical tile walls and a padded door to reduce distracting outside noises. The room will probably be sparsely furnished, containing only a desk-style polygraph, a swivel chair for the examiner, and a specially designed straight-backed interrogation chair for you.

Look around to see if there is a rectangular mirror set in one of the walls. If there is, you can conclude that it is actually a two-way mirror with an observation room on the other side. The observation room is exactly what the name implies —a chamber where other investigators or examiners can observe you without your observing them. They can listen, too

68

—for a microphone hidden in the interrogation room transmits to an amplifier-loudspeaker system in the observation chamber. One sales-minded owner of a polygraph service uses his observation room in a very practical way. He invites potential clients to watch actual job application interviews covertly from behind the two-way mirror. He reports that in almost every case the employer observes the fascinating goings-on with rapt attention, then proceeds to order polygraph examinations for his own new employees.

The examiner asks you to sit down. He keeps up a patter of friendly conversation, his voice calm and soothing, to relax you. Now he will explain that you have nothing to fear from the machine and that all you are required to do is tell the truth. He may repeat this several times for truth is, after all, the *raison d'être* for this whole situation.

But if you think you are to be immediately hooked on to the still-dormant polygraph you are mistaken. First (if you are taking the test as a condition of getting a job somewhere) comes a lengthy questionnaire. The examiner fills this out in longhand. Then he leads you through a rehearsal, giving you all of the test questions exactly as he will ask them during the actual examination. Though it's a dry run, many people break down at this point, confessing to sins—both petty and major—they feel will be elicited during the actual examination.

At last, the lie test itself. The examiner again tells you that you have nothing to fear as long as you tell the truth. He places your arms into two troughs that constitute the arms of the chair. He binds the pneumograph—a corrugated rubber tube that expands and contracts as you breathe—around your chest. This section of the apparatus will record your normal breathing rate and indicate changes in that rate. Next, he wraps an inflatable rubber cuff—the sphygmomanometer—around your upper arm. This nearly unpronounceable section records your pulse rate, pulse wave amplitude and relative blood pressure, as well as any changes that might occur in each. Finally, he attaches a couple of electrodes to your fingers. These lead to the galvanograph, which measures your skin's resistance to a weak electric current.

Thus bound, wrapped and attached, you are ready for the lie test. The examiner flicks a switch. The polygraph begins its dull whir. Your body impulses, fed into the polygraph via all those gadgets, emerge as jiggly lines on a moving roll of graph paper. If the lines remain in a fairly steady pattern while you are being questioned, you are likely telling the truth. Any noticeable deviation, however, could lead the examiner to interpret your answer as a lie.

Without exception the commercial polygraph examiners I interviewed were fervent believers in lie detection as *the* answer to any and all personnel problems. In their published writings they are similarly ecstatic and not at all averse to spreading the good word. One owner of a lie detection service, written up by the trade journal *Restaurant Management,* claimed a long list of benefits to be derived from the polygraph. Lie tests, he said, promote better employer-employee relations, keep workers honest, rehabilitate valued employees whose larceny might otherwise cost them their jobs, lower the cost of bonding employees, provide greater savings and lead to bigger benefits for employees.

As we shall see, however, not everyone considers the polygraph a boon to mankind. There is, for example, the truck driver who applied for a job as long-distance hauler and was informed he stood a good chance of being signed up but would have to go through a lie detector examination. He recalls, "They said they had an expensive training program and wanted to make sure I intended to stay on the job. I told them I sure would, but they wanted the test to back me up. So I took it. There were just a couple of questions about the job. The rest were personal as hell."

Late in 1962 some ladies in Hartford, Connecticut, had their own peculiar experience with some highly personal lie test questions. The ladies were applying for jobs in a pilferage-plagued department store which asked them to prove their own probity by taking polygraph examinations. Soon they discovered that the examiner had far more than pilferage on his mind, as they subsequently pointed out in angry letters to the Connecticut State Department of Labor. One woman gave an account of a portion of her test:

EXAMINER: Have you ever used intoxicating liquors or drugs?
WOMAN: Yes, iron pills.
EXAMINER: How do you feel?
WOMAN: Lousy.
EXAMINER: Are you pregnant?
WOMAN: No.
EXAMINER: Do you have your period?
WOMAN: No, I'm just sick and disgusted about the whole thing here.

In testing a teen-age girl who wanted to work in that

Hartford department store, the examiner apparently felt it his duty to protect the store—in advance—from any kind of scandal. A fragment of the examination allegedly went as follows:

EXAMINER: Do you go out with boys?
GIRL: Yes.
EXAMINER: Do your parents approve?
GIRL: Yes.
EXAMINER: Do you go too far with the boys?

The letter writer did not record the reply to that question, but I can report the reaction of an ethical examiner to whom I recounted this incident. He swore mightily, contending that such invasions of privacy give the whole profession a black eye. He may well be right, for in 1963 pressure was being put on the Connecticut state legislature (as well as the legislatures of New York and New Jersey) to ban the use of lie detectors by employers.

The Connecticut examiner, I am told, deviated from the standard line of questioning. What, then, are the standard questions asked in a pre-employment examination—the ones that presumably do not constitute an invasion of privacy?

Out of one such test, which covers 31 points, I have picked the following as representative:

Are you holding back information about a past mental ailment?

Are you holding back information about past or present marital problems?

Are you holding back information about a debt in which you are behind in your payments?

Are you holding back information about the actual amount of your gambling?

Are you holding back information about the actual amount of your drinking?

Has drinking caused you to lose at least one day's working time?

Are you holding back information about a theft from a former employer, fellow employee, or customer in which you have been involved?

Are you holding back information about a time you were arrested, questioned by the police, confined to jail or court-martialed?

Are you holding back information about an incident or condition which might open you to pressure or blackmail?

Are you holding back information about a lack of confidence to learn and perform the duties required of this new job?

Are you holding back information about something important concerning yourself not covered during this interview?

Are you holding back information about an accident you have had while driving?

Are you holding back information about a speeding or reckless driving ticket or license suspension?

Are you holding back information about being unwilling to report thefts committed by fellow employees?

The tenor of the questions makes them more suitable for a third degree than for application to a man or woman simply looking for a job. In fact, in a New York *Herald Tribune* series on the polygraph a number of years ago, some critics called the whole procedure the "fourth degree." In fairness to the profession, it must be said that every responsible examiner avoids that kind of atmosphere. He strives to seem the pleasant, friendly fellow, to inject an air of sincerity and sympathy into the proceedings—almost like a dentist reassuring his squirming patient that *really* it won't hurt. And, like the dentist, his purpose is to relax the person in the hot seat, thus making it easier for everyone concerned. Fear and nervousness, as the next chapter will show, can play havoc with a polygraph examination.

Executives undergoing lie tests are not always interrogated bluntly. Sometimes the line of questioning is woven subtly to develop specific attitudes or personality characteristics. An examiner working for a private detective agency cited three examples from recent interrogations. The first involved a New England executive whose firm wanted to transfer him to a branch plant in the South. Problem: did the manager harbor any antagonism toward the South and Southerners? The examiner eased into the subject gradually by talking first about a mythical friend of his who had been in a Southern state and supposedly hated it. The whole session was more like a conversation, relaxing the executive and giving the examiner a chance to observe his spontaneous reaction to the artificial situation.

The second case involved an account executive whose moral character had to be definitely established. The polygraph examiner casually asked the subject if he danced well. Then he asked if the executive danced only with his wife. When the answer was in the negative, the examiner created a fake situation involving himself and another man's wife. They had been dancing together, the examiner said, when the lady made it very obvious that she would welcome a more intimate relationship with him. Still embroidering on this phony incident, the examiner concluded by relating how he had met the woman some hours later and taken her to his apartment. At the end of his disarming tale he asked in an offhand manner, "Guess you would have done the same in a case like that?" The subject assured him he would indeed have done the same—and by the candid answer probably sandbagged his chance for advancement.

The third example recounted by the examiner involved a vice-president being considered for a position in which company policy would depend largely on his judgment. Main purpose of the examination was to probe, in every way possible, the extent of the man's inner security. In his easygoing way, the examiner brought conversation around to the vagaries of the stock market. "That man was so worried about our economy," he reported, "that I had to conclude he was too scared to make a major decision."

It is difficult to grasp the overpowering effect the polygraph has on most people unless one participates directly— either as a subject or participant. While researching this book I observed an actual pre-employment lie detector test being given to a man who had applied for a really "sensitive" job— he was going to sell cheap rugs and other valuables in an upstate New York discount store. Later I learned that the owner of the store (he runs a chain) demanded lie tests on everyone who came to work for him, no matter how menial the job.

During the interrogation I perched on a stool in the observation chamber and peered into the interrogation room through a two-way mirror. The subject was a tall, thin, extremely nervous man in his middle thirties. He walked in literally quaking. The first thing he said was, "Ever since I heard I had to take the test I've been so nervous, I've been like this. . . ."

He held up his hands, which were trembling. The examiner remained unperturbed. He might have been a surgeon soothing a patient about to go on the operating table, or a chaplain calming a greenhorn soldier facing his first battle. He said, in a voice at once calm and firm, "There's nothing to worry about. We're going to go over the whole thing before you take the test. I'll help you all I can. If you tell the truth, you don't have to worry a bit."

The subject gave him a grateful look. Even so, he needed—and got—repeated assurances that everything was all right. The examiner took him over his background. The man's last job, before he was laid off, had been as home-delivery route driver for a bakery. Suddenly he blurted, "I'm high-strung, my doctor told me I was, and I've been thinking deeply about this—I mean, it *is* stealing. I don't mean I took truckloads. Just a loaf of bread from the truck on the way home. Petty stuff. But when you get down to it, it *is* stealing."

It took me an instant to realize that the testing situation had led him to make an abrupt confession of a petty theft even before he was hooked up to the polygraph.

For his part, the subject now looked cowed, the prisoner hoping for a reprieve but not really expecting to get it. The examiner merely shrugged. In a fatherly voice he said, "Everybody's done something minor. We'll discuss it, get it out real fast, and forget about it."

The subject licked his lips and nodded, clearly relieved. It was hard to recall, at least for me, that the man there wanted just an ordinary job.

The interrogation went on. Earlier jobs, more confessions. Once he brought home an occasional bottle of soda water; another time he stole candy bars from a packing case to munch on at lunchtimes; he took a flashlight from a gas station that had employed him; on still another vending route he had shortchanged an occasional customer he did not like, but insisted he had never made a practice of that.

The owner of this polygraph service tiptoed into the observation chamber to see how I was enjoying the spectacle. During our earlier chats he had impressed me as a warm, friendly individual. He whispered, "Fascinating, isn't it?"

I had to admit that it was, resisting the impulse to add that I would not want to go through such a test myself.

"I never grow tired of watching," he confessed. "Here you really see human nature on display."

"Will they hire that guy?" I wondered.

"Probably. If it doesn't get too bad."

"Clients don't care about this petty stuff?"

"Some do, some don't," the owner replied. "If they want a man who's one hundred percent clean, they'll have to do a lot of looking. Ninety percent of the people we test have taken *something*."

We turned back to the interrogation. The subject was still

74

explaining some little trifle he had put into his pocket. I wondered if all these small confessions were like pebbles rolling down a hillside, with the huge boulder about to come crashing down. But there was none of that. He emphatically denied ever having gone in for organized stealing, ever taking merchandise for the purpose of selling it.

"I wouldn't have the nerve," he said. "I'm shaking inside, but I hope that shows up on the test."

When the dry run was finished, the pneumograph was wrapped around his chest, the electrodes attached to his fingers. (This time the sphygmomanometer was not used.) The actual lie test was at hand. The subject looked stricken. I noted, with some surprise, that my own throat was dry.

Seeking for the hundredth time (or so it seemed) to reassure his frightened subject, the examiner said gently, "See? The questions are easy."

"Yes, but I don't know about my insides," muttered the man.

"Don't worry about your insides as long as you're telling the truth."

This didn't seem to have the desired effect. Breathing heavily, the subject said, "I'm actually shaking."

By now the apparatus was on and whirring. For a few moments the examiner bent over the pens that were tracking up the moving graph paper. At last he was ready. His tone a trifle more formal, he began the questioning. Each time the subject gave his answer there was a pause. Each time the needle seemed to jump. Frequently the examiner penciled a notation directly on the graph paper. Mercifully, the subject was unaware of all this. Following instructions, he stared straight ahead at a point on the wall. I strained to see the graph paper, but it was beyond my field of vision. Was the man lying? Were those pen jumps significant? I turned to ask the owner of the agency, but he had stepped out without my hearing him.

The examiner neared the end of the questioning. Still the tension kept mounting. At last came the final question. It was given, answered in the negative (as were all the others), and the whole thing was over.

The examiner switched off the apparatus. "You did fine," he told the subject, "just fine."

The subject gave a long sigh. His face took on a little more life as he watched the pneumograph and the electrodes being removed from his body. He said, "I don't think I'll ever forget this." That was understandable. It had been quite an experience for a man who just wanted to sell cheap rugs in a discount store. But he had done well, despite all his confessions. When he had gone, the examiner telephoned the client and recommended him.

7. The Lie Detector:

Industry's Electric Chair

Part Two

A FEW YEARS ago a restaurateur in North Carolina tired of losing money on light-fingered employees working in his steak house. To remedy the situation he brought in a lie detector and subjected everyone on the payroll to it. The thefts stopped. Other restaurant owners in the area were so impressed they asked him to give lie tests to *their* workers. Pretty soon the steak house owner realized he had gotten hold of something live and went into the polygraph field fulltime. According to *Restaurant Management*, which told his story, in short order over 100 businesses of all kinds signed up as clients.

Such success stories thrill the polygraph industry, which commands from $25 to $50 for each pre-employment or periodic lie test, and $50 up for each employee tested in an actual theft case. Nevertheless, the polygraph consistently arouses as much ire as enthusiasm—making it, as *Business Week* has pointed out, "one of the most controversial tools" used in corporate security.

The morality of giving blanket lie tests to prospective or existing employees is often questioned. For instance, New York State Senator Thomas Laverne, who sponsored, unsuccessfully, a bill to outlaw employers' use of the polygraph in his state, demanded, "If an employer may use the lie detector test, cannot it be said that he can also use psychoanalysis, hypnosis or truth serum to learn the inner workings of his employee's mind?"

By no means are only outsiders critical of the current trend to commercialize the polygraph. Dr. Joseph F. Kubis, a professor of psychology at Fordham University, has worked with the lie detector since 1936, aided in its development, conducted a number of polygraph studies for governmental and scientific bodies, and administers polygraph tests in criminal cases. Yet Dr. Kubis feels the growing use of the lie detector in many vital aspects of daily life is "unwarranted, dangerous and degrading." Pointing out that indiscriminate use of the polygraph violates the basic dignity of man, he says, "I could see it for white rats. There has to be more than an economic reason for its use when other means of investigation could be used."

When I first began to explore the polygraph's rising appeal to businessmen, I did so mainly with the moral view in mind. What, I wondered, was the lie detector's impact on the already-precarious state of our privacy? However, it soon became clear that there were other considerations to take into account. These can be summed up in a single, all-important word: validity. It is far from certain that the lie detector always—or even most of the time—tells the truth. In fact, the polygraph industry finally seems like the man who, having unwittingly purchased a badly leaking sailboat, comforted himself with, "It's a great boat if you forget about the holes."

Unfortunately, the man or woman whose job and/or reputation depends on the outcome of his polygraph adventure cannot forget about the holes.

Any fair-minded observer would have to admit that within set limits the polygraph has had its share of successes, both in law enforcement and in the private field. As a result of lie tests, criminals have confessed, employees have admitted a history of pilferage, and unjustly accused persons have occasionally been cleared. Such successes, however, do not result solely from the polygraph findings. The highly skilled examiner is also an expert interrogator and adept at exploiting the psychological impact of the procedure. As we shall see, in less expert hands the entire procedure becomes a dangerously hit-or-miss proposition.

The powerful effect which the lie detector has on so many people is perhaps best illustrated by the increasing popularity of periodic testing. This means that employees are not only tested when they first come on the job but at set intervals thereafter. *Business Week* has quoted the president of Bramson's, a Chicago department store, as saying he cut his losses in half the first year after introducing periodic checks.

In order for the polygraph to work its psychological magic everybody concerned—both subject and employer—must be convinced of its infallibility. Examiners claim—if not total infallibility—at least near-perfection. Accuracy of 95 percent is the figure generally quoted in the field. Critics say no reliable evidence supports such a statistic—in the words of three psychologists writing in the *Harvard Business Review,* "There is nothing to document the claims to accuracy or effectiveness except bald assertions."

But never mind. Few employers and fewer employees are apt to have read that *Harvard Business Review* article. As far as they are concerned, the lie test cannot go wrong and when there is a dispute it is usually the subject who comes out the loser. One case involved an eighteen-year-old Texan who was given a lie detector test after money was stolen from his employer. The boy was so nervous that the test had to be temporarily called off. When it was finally given, the examiner told his client that the results were "inconclusive." Nevertheless, the boy was fired. The reliability of the test, even when it could not come up with clear-cut findings, was not questioned.

An even more frightening example of the harm wrought by an unquestioning belief in the polygraph comes from Drs. H. B. Dearman and B. M. Smith of the University of Virginia School of Medicine. In the case reported by these two doctors a polygraph examination erroneously showed a bank vice-president to be guilty of embezzlement and nearly ruined his career. The incident began when a routine polygraph examination was given all of the bank's personnel. When the vice-president was asked if he had ever stolen any money from the bank or its customers, he answered in the negative. However, the polygraph readings showed him definitely to be lying.

The bank's books were carefully audited. There was no shortage. The vice-president underwent a second lie detector examination. Again the test showed him to be lying. But a second audit failed to turn up any shortage. The vice-president went through still another lie test. But by this time the pressure on him was too great and he "confessed" to having stolen money, even making up a method by which he took the cash.

Nevertheless, a third audit of the books failed to turn up evidence of wrongdoing. The president of the bank, at the end of his tether, sent his harassed official to psychiatrists. Eventually they discovered that he had really never taken a cent from anyone. He had triggered off a "false positive" reaction because of unconscious hostilities involving his wife and his mother, both of whom were customers of the bank.

If unconscious hostilities can create test patterns indicative of lying, can other emotions do the same? Simple fear solely engendered by the prospect of having to take a test, for instance? The answer is a resounding yes. *Police,* a slick monthly for law enforcement officers, advises: "The success of a test depends in part on how the person was treated before he was asked to take the test, how he was asked to take the test, and how he was treated while awaiting the test." Employers are usually advised to soft-pedal the announcement that a lie test must be taken, but not everyone follows instructions. One commercial polygraph organization wondered why so few job applicants were showing up for tests ordered by one particular client—and why the ones who did come seemed excessively nervous. Later it discovered, to its dismay, that the client was telling his prospective employees, "We want to catch the thieves before they come to us."

But fear is far from the only factor that can cause polygraph readings suggestive of deception. A polygraph examiner with the Long Beach, California, Police Department, stated in the Sept./Oct. 1961 issue of the *American Journal of Correction:* "A person entirely innocent of the offenses for which he is being examined can be so angered at being inconvenienced, or angered at even being suspected, that he can under examination with the polygraph show on his chart deviations identical to those of deception. Hate can do the same."

It is not too farfetched to assume that a job applicant facing the polygraph ordeal may also feel anger, resentment— even hate. Assuming he has no preconceived resentment, the line of questioning itself can easily bring it on. Dr. Kubis points out that "fishing expeditions"—in which the applicant is bombarded with emotionally charged questions—may be subject to misinterpretation by the examiner.

Not only attitudes and emotions but the physical condition of the person taking the lie detector test plays a role in his responses. *Police* lists the following mental and physical characteristics that may affect a person's reactions during the test: certain heart conditions; certain breathing disorders; highly nervous or excitable states; dope addiction; chronic alcoholism; illness or pain; extreme physical or mental fatigue; colds; coughing spells, hay fever, asthma and the like; insanity; mental deficiency; improper treatment or questioning prior to taking the test.

Quite a list.

The polygraph industry contends that a skilled examiner takes all of these factors into account when administering the test and interpreting it's results. It describes the polygraph as nothing more than a diagnostic tool whose reliability depends entirely on the man who uses it. This makes sense. Let's accept the fact that a highly experienced examiner can weed out physically unfit subjects, relax the others, differentiate between true deception and emotions like fear or anger, and can somehow even take unconscious hostilities into consideration (though it hardly seems likely). A pertinent question follows. Is the average person going through a lie detector examination in business and industry apt to encounter such a paragon?

The answer comes from the experts themselves. In 1961 James V. Bennett (Director, U.S. Bureau of Prisons), made this frank statement in the *American Journal of Correction:* "From various persons who are intimately acquainted with the polygraph field, I have elicited an opinion of the number of qualified examiners there are in this country. Most of them estimated about half-a-dozen." He added that one "charitable correspondent" thought there might be two dozen, the highest estimate he received.

In 1963 a ranking polygraph examiner for a New York agency told me, "I wouldn't trust more than three examiners in the U.S. to give me a polygraph test." Even as firm a polygraph believer as Leonard Lowell admitted disgustedly, "There are a lot of quacks in the business."

Largely responsible for this state of affairs is the almost incomprehensible fact that hardly any state requires polygraph examiners to be licensed. As this book was written, responsible examiners in Illinois, New York and elsewhere were prodding their state legislatures to pass licensing laws, but only a single state—Kentucky—actually had one on the books. It is by no means certain that any other state will follow suit. This means every person who wants to can plunk down from $250 to $1,400 for a polygraph and set himself up in business—notwithstanding the fact that he may have stopped going to school in the fifth grade, or spent half his life in prison, or learned to operate the machine from an instruction booklet thoughtfully provided by the manufacturer. He may also have been fired for corruption or incompetence by a legitimate lie test firm, then set up shop on his own. A few polygraph examiners so discharged are actually competing in the same cities with the firms that got rid of them.

Training is another controversial point, one that renders the polygraph industry vulnerable. A Burns examiner told me he was greatly worried about the future of the polygraph field because he considers training methods woefully inadequate. One Chicago school for polygraph examiners has a six-month training course. Many other courses last six weeks or less—six weeks to study psychology, physiology, interrogation techniques and the mechanics of the machine itself. Field work on actual cases? No time for that, in many instances. In at least one school the student examiner works his field cases *after* he is out on his own, sending a number of completed cases back to the school for evaluation. Then, if he did a good job of interpretation on 25 cases or so, he receives his certificate of completion. His subjects have no idea, of course, that they are guinea pigs for an examiner who has not even graduated yet.

Dr. Kubis would like to see all polygraph examiners university-trained, with a degree in psychology and an extensive one-year apprenticeship with a qualified examiner, before they go out on their own. This hardly seems too much to ask when the subject is required to lay his job, his reputation, and maybe his freedom on the line. McKesson & Robbins has stated that polygraph tests for its employees are given by staff members with college degrees in psychology. This is rare. Most business and industrial concerns using lie tests do not have staff examiners and few independent examiners are bona fide psychologists.

Examiners are not only critical of each other's ethics and training but of the apparatus itself. One lie detector on the market tests only for galvanic skin response. (You can buy a toy version of it for about $25.) The machine is cheap and is used by some budget-minded police departments, a number of lesser-known private detective agencies and a few industrial security departments. Few of the examiners I interviewed were enthusiastic about it. One condemned it outright. But it probably makes as much of a psychological impact as the expensive and refined polygraphs manufactured by Associated Research Inc., and C. H. Stoelting, the two leaders in the field.

Some few examiners—notably the late Leonarde Keeler—have made serious attempts to raise the standards of the polygraph industry, improve training and technique, and reduce the danger of erroneous interpretation. But though the polygraph has been used for decades, its findings still are not admissible in courts of law. (Confessions gained as a result of lie tests, on the other hand, are admissible.)

So tricky and complex is this business of interpreting lie test patterns correctly that the Air Force commissioned Fordham University to conduct a study on the feasibility of using computers instead of human examiners to do the interpreting. Completed in 1962 by Dr. Kubis, the study notes that at present the examiner "makes his measurement by eye, his evaluation by an inner mental weighing process, and his decisions, in large part, by experiential intuitions and hunches. *This is a far cry from the scientific reputation often accorded the lie detection process.*" (Italics mine.) The study, significantly enough, showed that at present the human element is still so variable, it is impossible to program a computer to make polygraph evaluations.

An interesting facet of the Air Force study involved ways in which subjects could "beat the machine," as one examiner described a jamming operation. He contended that, given an experienced examiner, it was virtually impossible for anyone to outfox the procedure. Yet the study showed that subjects could indeed train themselves to jam the apparatus in such a way "as to deceive and confuse the lie detection operator in his evaluation of the records." One way, according to the study, is to learn how to tense certain muscles, such as toe muscles, which cannot be easily detected by the examiner. Another effective way is to use "exciting imagery"—in other words, the subject reproduces a mental image that gets him excited or upset and throws off the test pattern.

Examiners not only have the job of objectively evaluating lie test patterns, they must also decide what to tell the prospective employer and what to omit. Yes, some thoughtful examiners do not always test and tell. Polygraphist Richard C. Arther, who once candidly informed a class of embryo examiners that "you've got a lot of responsibility because you're judge, jury and law enforcement agency all at once," told me he keeps derogatory information from a client if the subject transgressed in his extreme youth and did nothing antisocial in the intervening years. Other examiners have indicated they do the same thing. Still, with less than 10 percent of some 600 examiners said to be qualified, it may safely be imagined that most are only too happy to transmit to their clients every minute speck of derogatory information that comes up.

What happens to the independent soul who, revolted by

82

the idea of having to take a polygraph test, declines the offer? Obviously, he cannot be compelled to go through with the procedure. But just as obviously, the coercive element is implicit in the process. If a prospective employee refuses to take the lie test—even when it is merely "suggested" that he take one—it is not difficult to imagine that he will remain prospective. If someone already on the payroll refuses, it may be taken for granted that his presence at work will no longer be welcomed. If he is hardy enough to decline to take a test in a specific theft situation, it is plausible to assume that he will at once become a prime suspect.

In this connection there was an informative exchange between Adison Verrill, president of Dale Systems, Inc., and a whimsical Connecticut lawmaker, Rep. E. Badalato. The occasion was a March 1963 Connecticut State Labor Committee hearing to consider bills that would outlaw the use of lie detectors by employers as a condition for getting or keeping a job.*

REP. BADALATO: You stated that you didn't believe that anyone would be discharged because they refused to take the lie detector test; do you also feel that any new applicant to a position would be hired if he refused to take a lie detector test?

MR. VERRILL: Would they be hired?

REP. BADALATO: Would they be refused employment if they refused to take a lie detector test?

MR. VERRILL: This is the type of question that I couldn't answer because, not being an employer . . . but I would say this . . . that we tell employers when the tests are given that they cannot refuse to hire a person because they refuse to take the test . . . or if it is on a specific . . . if there was a theft of cash from an office of which five people could be involved, if four people agree to take the test and the fifth doesn't we tell the employer you cannot discharge the individual because of their refusal to take the test.

REP. BADALATO: Have you ever tested the employer to find out if that was why they refused to hire possibly that one employee that did not take the test?

MR. VERRILL: Have we ever tested an employer?

REP. BADALATO: To find out whether that was the reason why they did not. . . .I think it would be a good test.

* Massachusetts is the only state that actually has passed such a law.

83

MR. VERRILL: If they would pay for it . . . we would be happy to.

Here this line or questioning was dropped. It is safe to assume that neither Mr. Verrill's organization nor any other polygraph service would ever earn a cent on the basis of Rep. Badalato's suggestion. Connecticut's Labor Commissioner Renato E. Ricciuti was one of the individuals who testified on behalf of the proposed ban-the-polygraph bills. Ricciuti told me that after complaints began to come to the Labor Commission it tried to dissuade several employers from giving lie tests. The Commission was unsuccessful. He finds that some people would rather quit their jobs than go through the pressure of a test.

Coupled with the pressure, of course, is the danger that if there is an erroneous finding of guilt it will be placed in the employee's personnel folder to haunt him for the rest of his working life.

Not surprisingly, examiners show little sympathetic understanding about the rising pressure to outlaw polygraph tests for industrial use. One of the most vociferous opponents of the Connecticut bill was Lincoln Zonn, member of the National Board of Polygraph Examiners and owner of a private testing firm. Testifying at the Connecticut hearing, he stated, "Gentlemen, my personal opinion—there are certain subversive elements that would be tickled pink to see Legislation like this passed because the Government does use it extensively to ferret them out."

Maybe so. Still, there are two points to keep in mind: 1) the Government's use of it was not at issue in the hearing; 2) law enforcement agencies use many other resources that are not—and should not be—available to private parties.

Fundamental issues are at hand in employee testing, I think, but they do not concern subversion. Perhaps those issues are best framed in the form of questions. Are the American people really ready to stand before judge and jury as a prerequisite for exercising their right to work? Are they willing to submit to a procedure once reserved for criminal suspects—a procedure that is of doubtful validity, that humiliates the subject and degrades the very essence of his privacy, that by its nature presumes him guilty, forces him to testify against himself, and allows him no defense—even when the test is conducted by the most sympathetic and skillful of examiners? Is management ready to embrace a screening system that will inevitably come to be known as a symbol of suspicion and distrust?

Are you?

8. Big Brother on the Job

SUCCESSFULLY NEGOTIATING THE hiring procedure—with or without polygraph—by no means makes it certain that the employee is out of the investigative woods. On the contrary, investigators (both human and electronic) may play fast and loose with his privacy each and every working day. In an effort to spot dishonesty, promote courtesy, and get a line on what their managers and workers are thinking and saying, thousands of American factories, offices, mercantile organizations and warehouses spy upon their own. The range, the techniques, the volume of all this sleuthing is both dismaying and fantastic.

The firms that have institutionalized surveillance techniques of one kind of another justify the intrusion by quoting a few statistics culled from insurance companies, the American Society for Industrial Security, the National Retail Merchants Association, and other sources. The statistics relate to employee dishonesty and they numb the senses. Every single year thieving workers make off with at least $1 billion in cash and merchandise. Every single day white collar workers steal about $4 million. In 1961 alone, an insurance company has estimated, 1,195 businesses failed due to sustained losses caused by dishonest employees. In 1961, according to the *Wall Street Journal*, department, grocery, variety and discount stores lost some $714,000,000 due to pilferage (by both employees and customers), a rise of 41 percent from 1951.

Sometimes the theft habit becomes so ingrained, the culpable workers no longer consider what they are doing as dishonest. Pinkerton's broke a case like that. Employees of a wholesale grocery firm had been exchanging food from the different departments for so long, they considered this pilferage as a kind of "fringe benefit."

At first glance it would seem that anything management does, any weapon it uses to fell this demon of dishonesty that seems to have possessed so many, so much the better. Even if those weapons consist of the ultimate in intrusive devices and techniques. But this snap conclusion may have the edge taken off it just a bit by the consideration of three other points: 1) too often the intrusive weapons are preferred to other—in the long run more effective—programs of theft control; 2) too often the weapons are used in non-theft situations—applied for purposes that render their use reprehensible; 3) too often, even in actual cases of theft, they are used so indiscriminately they turn out to do more harm than good.

What happened to Chas. Pfizer & Co. some years ago illustrates the third point. Pfizer—one of our biggest manufacturers of drugs and pharmaceuticals—found itself in real trouble. Highly confidential process information was being leaked to another pharmaceutical company. Deeply and justifiably concerned, Pfizer officials determined to plug up the leak. They went about this task by instituting one of the most sweeping investigations ever conducted by a private firm. *Fortune* writer Richard Austin Smith correctly labeled it a "spy hunt." It was a wholesale prying into the personal lives of several hundred unsuspecting—though suspected—employees. Pfizer & Co. even went so far as to hire a professional eavesdropper who, along with several companions, was operating a wiretap factory in midtown Manhattan. So extensive were its facilities, the tappers potentially could listen in on conversations over an incredible 100,000 telephones.

With these facilities, the tapper was eminently equipped to perform the task Pfizer & Co. had in mind for him. He tapped many of the company phones used by Pfizer employees. He tapped the home phones of a number of employees. Remarkable for his thoroughness, he even tapped the phone belonging to the drug firm's general counsel *and* the phone of the company's outside counsel in Delaware.

This gross invasion of its employees' privacy cost the pharmaceutical house some $60,000 and gained it little in return. The guilty workers weren't uncovered. Subsequently, the tapper himself was arrested and convicted of violating the state wiretap laws. One of the many interesting disclosures made at his 1955 trial was that he had in his employ several men who were moonlighters of sorts. Their regular jobs were, conveniently enough, with the New York Telephone Company. These men made the actual taps.

Naturally, the New York Telephone Company waxed indignant over this unauthorized use of its men and its lines. Clearly, the company—and the public—had been victimized. The guilty workers were immediately fired. This spirited defense of privacy by the telephone company seems somewhat less impressive in the light of subsequent events. Testimony before the New York Joint Legislative Committee to Study Illegal Interception of Communications revealed that conversations between the employees and customers of the telephone company have been monitored by means of tiny microphones concealed in pen sets. Next time you drop by your local telephone company service representative, maybe you too will have a chance to say a few words into the mike. Lest you look askance at the practice, however, be advised that at the New York hearings telephone company officials claimed the purpose of the eavesdropping was to check up on the kind of service being given the paying customer.

The subject of electronic eavesdropping will be explored more fully in a subsequent chapter. But it must be noted here that electronic snooping devices have become standard fare with all kinds of intrusion-minded businesses from one coast to the other. At a 1959 wiretap hearing by the Senate Subcommittee on Constitutional Rights, former Philadelphia district attorney Samuel Dash told Senators the rationale behind all this enthusiasm.

"Once the industrialist or the plant owner started," Mr. Dash explained, "his appetite was whetted. When he saw the results that he could get through eavesdropping, that is. Very often, his purpose was to his mind legitimate, protecting his investment. There was no limit to what he would do. He was sold on the devices. He was sold on the expert who was working for him. He would tap the home phones [of employees], tap a competitor's phone, or tap in his own plant."

Mr. Dash spoke out of knowledge gained in conducting a comprehensive study of eavesdropping devices and their use, a study sponsored by the Pennsylvania Bar Association Endowment under a $50,000 grant from the Fund for the Republic. Many of the findings were later incorporated in a book, *The Eavesdroppers,* which offered some startling insights in the mores of the Goldfish Age.

In staid old Boston, says *The Eavesdroppers,* "a number of business houses employ concealed microphones in and around their plant or office to detect pilfering or to check up on employee loyalty and efficiency."

In Los Angeles, a wiretap expert has admitted installing 39 microphones in one large business organization alone. Each microphone was placed in a different department. Monitoring took place in the boss's office. You can imagine this man, flicking switches at will—each flick allowing him to listen in on a different set of conversations between and among his various unenlightened employees. There was a purpose behind the gentleman's peculiar penchant for auditory Peeping-Tomism. He wanted to find out what his employees were saying about him. It would be easy to guess what they might have said—well away from those mikes, of course—if they knew about his fun-and-games.

In San Francisco, a restaurant was found to have tiny microphones hidden underneath the customers' tables. The owner claimed that his only interest lay in making sure his waitresses were courteous.

The manager of a Philadelphia department store was so curious about the private lives of his large staff, he arranged to have all of the *public* pay phones in the building tapped. Any outside calls, whether made by employees or customers, were captured on automatic recording equipment located in the basement.

New York City was and is the wiretap center of the nation. Washington, D.C., probably runs it a close second. *The Eavesdroppers* notes that electronic eavesdropping has been going on in the New York area under the "direction and authorization of respectable and responsible business concerns. This eavesdropping has been internal in nature and has been used for purposes of store and plant security and checks on personnel. Its employment has become increasingly popular among business executives."

And in his testimony before the Senators, Mr. Dash made the pertinent comment that "this is being done, this is all being done through private detectives and specialists who sell a bill of goods to these industrial concerns that they can save thousands of dollars of money by checking on their own employees. This is a lucrative field for the specialist."

The more complex the job, the greater the rewards. Some eavesdropping installations get to be tremendously complicated. *The Reporter* has told of a West Coast wiretapper who installed an elaborate electronic eavesdropping system for the manager of an eastern aircraft factory. The manager quickly solved his immediate problem—namely, confirming his suspicion that dishonest purchasing agents were cheating the company out of substantial amounts. Some people might feel the situation justified the use of an investigative technique as pernicious as electronic eavesdropping. Typically, however, righteous motives for such spying soon turn more insidious. Observe what happened next.

What happened is that the manager went crazy about his electronic setup. He ordered a permanent surveillance system to maintain constant watch over the company's employees. The specialist installed four "bugs"—hidden microphones— in the men's washroom; two more in the women's washroom; another six in the company dining hall. A wiretap network covered all of the company's foremen, all of the department heads, five of the plant manager's top assistants. All the wires led to a control panel in the manager's office.

The specialist later recalled, "That's one factory where nobody pulls the wool over the boss's eyes. The manager found the setup very useful. He knows just which employees are acting up on the outside. He knows which junior executives are loyal to him and which are his enemies, and that way he knows who to promote and who to fire."

I related this incident to another manager, a high-level executive in an aerospace plant. His reaction was one of profound disgust. "That's security with a vengeance," he commented. "More to the point, it's total insecurity. To get the kind of control he wants over his people, he might try instituting weekly sessions of narcoanalysis." He pondered for a moment, then added, "Anyway, he couldn't keep his electronic setup a secret forever. That kind of thing gets around. After a while, do you know who would be his 'loyal' employees? The careful ones."

Coming increasingly into favor in plants is another electronic device—closed-circuit TV. Numerous factories have installations that monitor all entrances and exits, enabling security headquarters to screen everyone entering or leaving the premises. But this is an invention ideally suited for the surveillance of employees, and it is finding increasing application in just that way. Hidden closed-circuit TV cameras are to be found in shipping, warehouse and assembly areas. The employees in the surveillance area have no idea, of course, that their every move is secretly observed during the entire working day. Similar systems have been set up in department stores, to observe pilfering employees and customers. A measure of the popularity enjoyed by closed-circuit TV may be gained from the fact that in the 18 months after a system costing less than $1,000 was first introduced, over 30 private firms in the New York area alone snapped it up.

Even the final refuge of privacy—the company washrooms —are turning out to be no refuge at all. Both hidden mikes and two-way mirrors are being installed in them. A smiling investigator told me, "There's something about toilets that promotes a frank and hearty exchange of ideas among employees." Two-way mirrors, incidentally, are often installed in department store dressing-room areas to detect shoplifting by customers and stealing by employees.

Though usually not hidden in washrooms, flesh-and-blood investigators nevertheless perform a great variety of services for the firms that take an inordinate interest in their employees' activities. Nor is their presence always kept a secret. This is particularly true when it comes to the investigative service known as "shopping," which is probably the mildest form of internal snooping. "Shoppers" are men and women who pose as legitimate customers for goods and services; actually they rate employees' courtesy, efficiency and—mainly—honesty. Several investigative agencies, among them Willmark Service and Dale Systems, specialize in this type of sleuthing. *The Investigator's Handbook,* a how-to volume for tyro private eyes, explains that a shopper may, in the course of a day's work, "find himself in a branch of Woolworth's or some other chain, a vegetable store, gasoline station, automobile supply store, motion picture theatre, drugstore, etc. In fact, the list of businesses he may encounter is almost limitless. But the shopper's objectives are similar in every establishment." The book candidly continues, "In the opinion of the men who operate these shopping services, almost every employee will steal if afforded the opportunity. There is no 'trusted' worker."

To keep the worker on his toes, and his fingers off the merchandise, a goodly number of establishments mention in their welcoming speech to new employees the fact that shoppers will come around from time to time. Many have plaques in their establishments reading, "Serviced by . . . . . ." Bullock's Department Store in Los Angeles has even invented a "Mystery Shopper," an investigatory Santa Claus who comes around once a year, incognito, during a specified period. Every clerk who is given an excellent report is rewarded with a silver dollar.

The *Wall Street Journal,* discussing courtesy campaigns, told of Cities Service Oil Co., which also rewards courtesy through the use of shoppers. Called "mystery riders," they roam through City Service's 37-state marketing area to see how station attendants handle customers. According to the business newspaper, a "bad report means a reprimand; a good one means the award of prize points redeemable like trading stamps." Continental Airlines recently employed Dun & Bradstreet to make a survey of its operations, then used the findings in magazine ads. Noting that the survey found

Continental's flight crews "very helpful," the ad went on to explain, "Unknown to Continental Airlines operating personnel, Dun & Bradstreet's trained researchers flew 68,382 miles over our routes. They checked every phase of our passenger service."

Outside and traveling salesmen, parcel and wholesale delivery truck drivers—these come in for attention of a more intensive sort. Some employers are apprehensive about the fact that such employees perform their tasks on their own, without being under supervision. Does the outside salesman have a little business on the side? Is he abusing the expense account? Does he actually speak with purchasing agents or merely leave his card with secretaries? Does he do some finagling with orders? Does he sell his firm's vital marketing data to competitors? As for the truck driver, does he steal some of the parcels he is supposed to deliver? Does he deliberately stay out after making deliveries to qualify for overtime? Does he load up with unchecked merchandise to sell below wholesale price to unauthorized dealers? This apprehension is not always unwarranted. There have been numerous cases of hanky-panky involving salesmen, and as for the trucking—here is one small indication of what is happening: during a 3-day industrial security seminar at Michigan State University in 1963, participants learned that some 86 percent of all parcel delivery truck drivers have stolen packages from their trucks.

When a company wants to check on the honesty of its salesmen and drivers, it usually does so in a very simple, direct way: it arranges with a private detective agency to have the employees surveilled—tailed or shadowed, if you will. All day long, as the employee makes his rounds, a couple of detectives are following him in a nondescript car. Some companies that make use of surveillance do so only when there is actually some suspicion of wrongdoing. Others make periodic checks of all their outside people, whether there is any provocation for it or not, on the off-chance that something might turn up. And there are firms not content with reports that begin and end with the workday. They want to know what their outside people are doing after hours, too.

A Los Angeles investigator provided me with a vivid account of the way one manufacturer in the area has his outside salesmen and sales executives routinely investigated. The example given concerned a construction-materials salesman named Ed, who was scrutinized on a once-a-year basis in the following, unbelievably thorough way:

91

One investigator ran a neighborhood check on Ed to find out if 1) he entertained extensively; 2) lived within his income; 3) moonlighted or perhaps ran a business of his own on the side; 4) showed an inordinate interest in alcohol, women, or the nearby race tracks.

A second detective pored over musty files in government buildings to see if Ed had been involved in bankruptcy proceedings, litigation, or criminal activity.

But Ed himself was the focal point of the investigation. For an entire week a surveillance was run on him. A pair of investigators picked him up as he left his house in the morning. They noted the length of time he spent with each of his business contacts, where and with whom he had lunch (names if possible; if not, physical descriptions), and details of any unauthorized stops Ed made during his sales rounds. At the end of the workday the detectives trailed him back home.

If he went anywhere in the evening, either alone or with his wife, the detectives were right behind him. If he stayed in, they waited in their car until the lights of his house went out before calling it a day.

As it turned out in this case, Ed was honest, loyal, hardworking and apparently quite moral. We can merely conjecture, of course, how honest, loyal and hard-working he would have remained had he known of the unremitting way in which his privacy was being invaded—both day and night.

With regard to after-hours' surveillance of an employee, a Pinkerton promotional brochure provides a rationale apparently acceptable to the clients for this service. "Very often the employee's behavior outside of business can have a serious effect on the performance of his duties on the job," the brochure explains. It then goes on to state that the agency can ascertain the whereabouts, movements, activities, associates and mode of living of any employee.

By no means is the slam-bang surveillance the biggest investigatory gun leveled at the man or woman on the job. Even more potent—and perhaps more ominous—is the investigator (of either sex) who is planted incognito in a plant or office, the undercover operative. He is exactly what the name implies, an investigator who looks, acts, works, like all the other employees except that he observes their every move. He is a spy.

Undercover agents first came to public attention—and fell into disrepute—during the more militant days of the labor-management conflict in the 1920's and 30's. They were used to supply reports on employee unrest and the work of union organizers in clients' plants. A number infiltrated to the top ranks of the labor movement. Testimony before the La Follette subcommittee investigating labor espionage disclosed that some of the spies were charged with even more aggressive union-busting activities. Pretending to be labor agitators themselves, they provoked incidents designed to give labor a black eye. Labor spying was subsequently declared illegal in most states and none of the big, reputable detective agencies formerly involved in the game, like Pinkerton's, will touch it.

This does not mean today's undercover agent is short of work. In fact, despite the ban on labor spying, his scope is broader than ever. He may be working in the guise of porter, clerk, assistant buyer, stockroom worker, draftsman, even vice-president. He may be put into a factory to finger a theft ring; he may be looking for embezzlement, safety violations, poor supervision, favoritism, conflicts of interest; he may, in newly acquired companies, look for inaccurate reports and resentment of the new parent corporation on the part of the old executives. He may also—and frequently does—report employee gripes and what the workers are saying about management.

It is perhaps a portend for the future that the *Wall Street Journal* has reported a tremendous increase in the business community's use of undercover agents over the past few years: for example, Burns is providing undercover agents for some 500 clients, up 60 percent from 1955; the Mark Lipman Service of Memphis did $250,000 worth of business in 1956, around $1 million in 1961; Norman Jaspan Associates, Inc., another firm supplying undercover personnel, had 400 clients for its undercover services in 1958 and a hundred more in 1961.

The number of undercover operatives they have on their payroll is a secret closely guarded by the agencies providing them. "A substantial number," a Pinkerton spokesman told me, while a Burns official told another interviewer a few years ago, in answer to the same question, "I couldn't give you an exact figure, but it's really a hair-raising number." What this means to you, obviously, is that you never know whether the person at the next desk or the next bench, the person you might even see socially, is a legitimate employee or a company spy.

One detective agency once had something of a record: 35 undercover men in one factory. None knew the identity of the others, and in the kind of grim humor to be found in the Goldfish Age they wrote reports criticizing each other's conduct. To prevent leaks, only one or two key managerial figures in a given plant know of the undercover agents' presence. "Mice"—as undercover people are known in the telephone industry—come on the job through regular channels. Sometimes an opening is created for them; more often they simply apply at the personnel office along with other applicants. Since the personnel manager himself usually has no idea what is going on, the undercover agent may be turned down. In that case, more are sent until one finally is hired.

Undercover spying does not necessarily stop at day's end. Operatives are encouraged to strike up friendships with their fellow employees, to have a beer, go to the movies, or even on a fishing trip with them.

A typical case in which undercover operatives were used began when a Long Island, New York, electronics firm suddenly made a disconcerting discovery. Large quantities of very valuable switches were disappearing. Losses had already gone beyond the $5,000 mark and were rising. Officials of the firm attempted to check the pilferage but failed. They turned to the Burns Agency for help.

Burns planted four undercover operatives in various capacities inside the factory. None of the operatives knew who the others were. They spent eight months on the job, narrowing down on some suspects, but getting no further toward solving the case. They were unable to trap these men or gather evidence of any kind. They uncovered just one concrete bit of information concerning the suspects—they were fond of fishing.

The switches were, of course, still disappearing. In desperation, Burns officials persuaded the client to take on still another undercover man. This one had a singular asset. He was a confirmed saltwater fisherman.

Using fishing as a bait, he hooked the suspects into a friendship with him. When summer came, the suspects invited the undercover man to join them on a fishing trip. The pungent aroma of freshly caught bass broiling in the pan must have loosened tongues. Assuming he was their buddy, someone they could trust, they told him in detail about their lucrative sideline of stealing switches.

Upon returning to work they began to steal for him as well as for themselves. They showed him the warehouse in which they kept the purloined gadgets. They even introduced him to the fence who disposed of the merchandise. Burns officials, working in conjunction with local police, set a trap for the thieving employees. The undercover man led them into it and the operation was safely concluded with the thieves' arrest.

The departure of an undercover agent is handled with as much of a cloak-and-dagger routine as his arrival. He does not simply pack up and go once the job is completed but remains working quietly for a month or two, then offers a plausible excuse for quitting. That way there is little likelihood for him to be connected with the breakup of the theft ring, and the possibly embarrassing fact that it has been using paid informers is kept a secret by the company.

Despite all the careful planning, however, sometimes a leak occurs. A woman who worked for a New York department store tells what happened after word got around that the store had been using undercover agents:

"At first we were all amazed. We'd never thought of anything like that. We wondered if those people were still with us. All of the salesgirls were nervous, in a giggly kind of way at first. People went around making jokes. 'Are you a spy?' one would say to the next. But that kind of thing wasn't really a joke and after a while we just looked at each other suspiciously. Wasn't a pleasant atmosphere to work in. Everybody started to watch what they were saying. I had the feeling somebody had their eyes on me all the time. I quit soon after."

By no means are undercover agents used only to solve specific problems. Many a mistrustful employer, perhaps as much enchanted with the idea of hiring detectives as by fear of robbery, uses undercover people as a kind of insurance that he will be able to spot potential trouble well ahead of time. In fact, D. Bruce Burns, vice-president of the Burns Agency, has said, "Many of our clients would no more think of discontinuing their undercover service than discontinuing fire or theft insurance."

A young man I knew on the West Coast was placed undercover as an order clerk inside a meat-packing firm as soon as he landed a job with a detective agency. A year later he was still there, comfortably ensconced in his dual role, filling orders and spying on his colleagues.

When he first began this job, his superior at the detective agency simply told him, "Keep your eyes and ears open— and report everything the boss might want to know." There was no specific problem to solve, nor did any kind of theft situation turn up during the twelve months he stayed there. No embezzlement, no kickbacks, no theft ring—nothing but a few minor cases of pilferage.

Every evening, he prepared a handwritten report on the day's activities. If nothing happened he said so, though sometimes he added a few harmless embellishments to make the client feel he was getting his money's worth.

At times his reports were more detailed. He quoted verbatim Employee X's disparaging remark about the boss. He noted Employee Y's critical attitude toward the food in the company cafeteria. He disclosed that Employee Z had begun taking a few nips from a pocket flask while on the job.

Once the report was completed, he shoved it into an envelope and dropped it into the corner mailbox. He did not know if anything was going to happen to Employees X, Y and Z. (He did discover that the food in the cafeteria became more palatable shortly after.) His report went to his superior at the detective agency, who edited it for grammar and spelling, had it typed, and forwarded it to the client.

My young acquaintance did not pursue the moral implications of his work. There are many ways of earning a living and this was his way. He enjoyed the glamour of being a private detective. He made good money—both the meatpacker and the agency paid him. If he had a couple of drinks with the boys—why, he got paid for that, too.

The moral implications do bother some Americans, who wonder what is happening to our traditional distaste for informers, paid or otherwise. Undercover operations may in certain situations be a necessary evil (even unions have agreed to their use in cases of high pilferage) but their routine use takes on a different cast entirely.

Industry is no more in agreement about undercover than it is about the polygraph. Some firms give it blanket endorsement. As *Fortune* has pointed out, others find the practice "repellent." In the middle is the group that believes undercover agents are of some value in specific cases, but would not use them merely as "insurance." Reflecting this middle group Russ White, G. E.'s security consultant, said, "Why not try to hire good solid citizens in the beginning, and then put some trust in them?"

This points up a curious and paradoxical situation. Companies using controversial techniques such as electronic eavesdropping and undercover justify themselves by the abysmal theft statistics, yet the business community as a whole has done precious little to stamp out the ever-growing wave of thefts. Investigative agencies and insurance companies that have to make up the losses are in virtual agreement about this. A crime expert from the Liberty Mutual Insurance Company has said, "There is no question that business could do plenty [about pilferage] if it only bothered. The carelessness is incredible. Many businessmen don't use plain common sense. They seem to go out of their way to invite crime. This indifference is peculiar."

The experts feel that these are some of the weak spots in management's struggle against theft:

Sloppy pre-employment screening. Despite the growing tendency to more stringent screening of prospective employees, many firms (especially in the merchandising fields) still do a quickie job of checking an applicant's background. Gaps in the employment record, not thoroughly investigated, sometimes hide prison terms or dishonesty in a previous employment.

Sloppy internal controls, poor plant or store protection. Tight internal controls may be expensive and troublesome to set up, plant procedures are often costly to install. Many firms are reluctant to pay the price. They prefer to write off a certain amount of pilferage by employees (or charge it off to the customer if possible). But this permissive attitude merely encourages more stealing, spiraling the losses to a still higher point.

Little or no prosecution of thieves. **Fortune** has pointed out that no system of prevention is worth much while management is tolerant toward the dishonest employees and "most companies today are still remarkably tolerant. The thief is usually fired, seldom prosecuted." If they prosecute, the victimized companies fear, they will get bad publicity. The public will hold them up to ridicule. They will lose face with the stockholders. The judge or jury will look with disfavor on a $6 million company prosecuting a worker who has taken $600 worth of goods. If the prosecution does not stick they run the risk of a damage suit.

Fortune tells of one nearly unbelievable case in which private detectives working on behalf of one company caught a thieving salesman. The company told this salesman it would not prosecute if, in return, he signed a confession that could be turned into the insurance company. The salesman came up with another proposition. He would sign the confession, he said—if he was not going to be required to make restitution, if he received a letter of recommendation, and if he got two weeks' severance pay. All three of his wishes were granted.

Writing in *Industrial Security,* Timothy Walsh points out that if employees know beforehand that a company will not prosecute, "the effect of fear of arrest and prison is lost." The effect of guards, alarms and pass systems is also weakened. As for the bad publicity in the press, Walsh feels this can be mitigated by effective public relations. With regard to the damage suit hazard, he adds, "If a security organization prepares the proper kind of case through approved investigative technique and careful fact gathering, and if actual arrest and confinement are left to the proper authorities acting in conformance with local statutory requirements, there is no reason to fear civil liability."

There are still other factors to consider regarding the employee thievery that invites so much on-the-job surveillance. There is not enough publicity about the theft problem. Its dimensions are such that the admittedly unsavory subject ought to be given as much of an airing as possible. The fact that Sylvia Porter, the financial columnist, made pilferage the subject of one of her columns in the summer of 1963 is an encouraging sign. Some newspapers editorialized on it. Expressing shock, the Salamanca, N.Y., *Republican Press* offered the constructive suggestion that "the implications of an annual billion-dollar loss from theft by employees ought to be studiously examined by churchmen, educators and others concerned with moral strength."

Newsweek, covering the security seminar at Michigan State, reported an equally sound suggestion by Donald R. Cressey, dean at the University of California at Santa Barbara. Cressey favored "a strong educational program. We've got to propagandize the fact that when you 'borrow' it you steal it . . . and when you steal it, you're a crook."

Basically, of course, employee dishonesty is only one phase of the breakdown of morality cutting across all aspects of American life today. The worker in the cosmetics factory who slips a few compacts into his pocket to give away to relatives (and eventually steals a much larger quantity for sale to a fence) does not live his life in total unsophistication.

He may not know that business kickbacks, payoffs and bribes are estimated at $5,000,000,000 a year—much of this going on at the supervisory or managerial level. He may not know that when one investigative organization uncovered dishonesties worth some $60 million in one year, it found that 62 percent of the losses were due to crooked supervisors and executives. He may not know that following the price-fixing convictions in the electrical industry, President Kennedy felt it necessary to appoint a committee of distinguished businessmen to serve as his Business Ethics Advisory Council.

He may not know all these things, but he has heard of

price-fixing, tax finagling, expense account chiseling, bribery and collusion. He has heard of advertising that misrepresents and he has heard about other forms of consumer fraud. If he is not cognizant of the details, he nevertheless has the vague but very real conviction that "they're getting theirs."

The corollary to that is, naturally, "I'll get mine."

So he steals—and so far the main attack on his dishonesty has been the use of hidden bugs, concealed TV cameras, tapped phones, two-way mirrors, sleuths and undercover agents in ever-greater profusion, which penalizes honest and dishonest employees alike.

Despite its illegality, the practice of labor spying persists. In fact, labor has learned a few tricks from management, and espionage now goes on in both directions. Giving the Senate Subcommittee on Constitutional Rights some of the details of his wiretapping survey, Samuel Dash told them, "It has expanded in the labor field as well where the labor unions are tapping the management and the management is tapping labor." He referred particularly to labor-management conferences. At a stage in the proceedings, he said, management walks out of the conference room, ostensibly for the purpose of allowing the union officials to talk things over among themselves.

"They usually walk to an adjoining room where they have a listening device connected to a bug in the discussion room," he went on. "They explain that what they did is not eavesdropping but that the labor people really have a problem they have not been able to communicate to management, that if they could listen to the conversation they could see where the real problem lies and go back and adjust it."

Most of the time the intrigue is not discovered, but occasionally a blatant case makes headlines. This happened in 1957 during a New York City subway strike. As a subsequent investigation developed, the New York Transit Authority (then owned by a private syndicate) had been spying on the Motormen's Benevolent Association (the strikers' union) for as long as 18 months—right up to the day of the strike.

The Transit Authority had secreted two microphones over the platform of the union's meeting hall. It had bugged the Times Square Hotel, also used by the union for conferences. On strike day it had even planted a detective inside a closet in the meeting hall from which he was able to watch the tableau through a peephole especially drilled for the purpose.

Labor mediators, too, have discovered that labor spying

still exists and that it has become a two-edged sword. For example, after attempting to settle a strike, mediator Cyrus Ching told friends his telephone lines were tapped by agents of both the company and the union.

However, labor spying need not involve outside sleuths. The Textile Workers Union finds that during organizing campaigns foremen are instructed by management to discover the identity of pro-union workers. The foreman will approach an employee and say, "I want you to tell me what the people in your car pool think about the proposed union."

Unions themselves are making use of other investigative techniques, particularly when negotiating time comes around. A New York investigator who insisted on anonymity told me of some of the jobs he has done for various labor unions throughout the country. On several occasions he has worked for unions which have been told by management, "We can't meet your terms, our business would be ruined." The investigator's job has been to find out exactly what kind of financial shape those businesses were really in—the behind-the-scenes information that financial books and statements do not necessarily reflect.

At other times union leaders have hired him to prepare "profiles in depth" of the management officials who would be sitting opposite them at the conference table. What the union leader wants to know about his opposite is, essentially, "What makes him tick?" The profile presumably gives him some idea of the businessman's quirks, prejudices—and weaknesses.

Of course, the management official has a similar dossier on the union man. Big Brother plays no favorites.

9. IE

THE CLOUDBEDS OF intrusion are further seeded by a segment of industry that spies not only upon its employees but upon itself. The practice is known as industrial espionage—or, more familiarly, IE. And IE is indeed becoming increasingly familiar. In 1959 *Time* noted, "Every U.S. businessman knows that espionage is as much a part of corporate competition as it is of international intrigue—but few have ever been willing to admit it." In 1962 a self-professed industrial spy was to tell me, "I have all the business I can handle. Demand for my services has increased one hundred percent in the last ten years."

In alarming measure, then, the most potent weapons in the investigatory arsenal are being used by the unscrupulous to snatch their competitors' brainchildren. The consequence is natural and inevitable. As businessmen watch the kidnap of vital research and marketing data, they recover from the shock to set up countermeasures employing equally potent devices of intrusion. The corporate arena becomes a hotbed of intrigue, on which writhe the forces of intelligence and counterintelligence. Ranged on the one side or the other are executives, salesmen, engineers, secretaries—as well as anyone else who, knowingly or not, gets in between the embattled opponents. And another nail is pounded into the coffin of workaday privacy.

The techniques of industrial espionage are as imaginative as those of international intrigue, though the victims are understandably lacking in appreciation for this particular creative effort. A New York food processor lost his secret—a coloring and flavoring agent he had developed—when a spy hired by one of his competitors paid a building superintendent a small sum for the daily accumulation of the food processor's wastepaper baskets. After carefully scanning the contents for three weeks running, the spy was able to piece together that vital formula.

A structural steel manufacturer consistently lost out on the largest bids. Finally becoming suspicious, he hired a private detective who discovered that all of the company's executive telephones were being tapped, presumably by the firm that always won the bids, though proof could not be obtained.

A chemical company forfeited some valuable research data when the competitor played the sex-trap game. First, private detectives prepared dossiers on a number of top executives on the staff of the target firm. Then one particularly susceptible executive was picked out as the most likely victim. Finally, a beautiful and—one may well imagine—excellently trained female spy arranged an "accidental" meeting with him. The meeting blossomed into an affair. Its final fruits were harvested by the competitive company as the industrial Mata Hari adroitly pumped her man for information.

This particular ploy—or a variation thereof—is a great favorite in other countries, too. Germany's Rosemary Nittbritt was a striking example. A prostitute upon whose life the film *Rosemary* was based, she catered to some of the biggest businessmen in Germany. Relaxing in her apartment, they often talked shop. Rosemary was a splendid listener. So was the recording equipment she had hidden all over her rooms. She made herself a tidy sum selling the tapes to her clients' competitors until, in 1957, she was murdered.

Surveillance is another common espionage technique. There have been cases in which a firm's ranking executive has been trailed the entire length of a round-the-world business trip. The men who tagged after him were thus able to determine his newest sources for sales or supplies. Conversely, foreign manufacturers are sometimes shadowed as they make their U.S. visits—by private detectives whose clients are anxious, suspicious local distributors fearful of being dropped.

Bribing is equally common. This may be petty: as when a supermarket regularly gives a printer $10 for advance information on the throwaway being printed for a competing supermarket. In certain situations hotel bellhops are bribed for a quick look at incoming and outgoing telegrams. A 1959 Harvard Business School study on IE—the most comprehensive study of its kind—noted with a deceptive lack of emphasis, "Some employees supplement their income by selling confidential information to competitors." In the Pinkerton files there is the story of the oil company switchboard operator who sold confidential lease-buying information—which she gained by eavesdropping on telephone conversations—to a curbstone broker who then snapped up the leases for himself. The case is far from unusual. Workers who could be "reached" have caused plenty of firms to lose millions of dollars' worth of research data. A notable example is provided by the American Cyanamid Company. In 1962 it launched a $15,000,000 suit charging that a former employee and a chemist working in the chemical company's Lederle division stole secret documents dealing with Aureomycin and other drugs, microfilmed them, and sold them to three Italian firms —netting from $50,000 to $60,000 from each firm.

When industrial spy Ulmont O. Cumming was hired by one firm to determine the ingredients used by another processor, he spent several days roaming the bars and lunchrooms in which the processor's employees hung out. Without much trouble he found an employee who would, for a price, bring him a sample of the ingredients.

Cumming has been characterized as "the nation's No. 1 industrial spy." Though he deprecates this designation, he did remark, when I interviewed him for a magazine article, "There isn't a plant I haven't gotten into."

Many a plant official has led the balding, ruddy-complexioned Cumming through his premises unaware of the master spy's true purpose. Cumming may have posed as a trade magazine writer wanting to do a story on the firm. Or as a stockholder interested in going through the plant in which he supposedly owned some shares. He may have been that quiet gentleman who accompanied the building or fire inspector on his rounds. He may have been the man in civilian clothes who was with the two police officers as they went through the factory "on a tip" looking for a robbery suspect. He may simply have been that grease-stained truck driver "mistakenly" sent to pick up a package.

Cumming, as all this suggests, is a master of impersonations. He chooses his roles carefully, reasoning them out to fit the particular situation, and plays them to perfection. He says, "Appearances are a big help in this business. You've got to able to make people believe you are what you say you are. You've got to be a good salesman."

He was an excellent salesman the time he was hired to find out certain marketing data only top-echelon executives of the victim firm would know. He posed as an executive recruiter, ostensibly interviewing those executives for more lucrative jobs elsewhere. Those phony interviews provided him with all of the information he needed to complete his assignment.

Spies like Cumming waste no time on painful introspection about the morality of their work. Theirs is a highly lucrative profession. Their pride finds its wellspring not in the job but in the job well done irrespective of obstacles. Cumming himself has said, with justice, "Some of the biggest companies in the U.S. engage in industrial espionage. If they're not worried about the ethics of the job, why should I be?"

Despite its present-day prevalence, industrial espionage has been around a long time. As far back as the seventeenth century, the British succeeded in making off with several German pottery-glazing techniques. Nevertheless, it has remained for our time to develop such a need for industrial spies that, as *Fortune* has pointed out, many FBI, OSS, CIA, Signal Corps and military-intelligence men have left "to set up shop as independent operators" in the IE field, where the pay is much more substantial.

Newsweek has explained that to a certain extent this frenetic snooping is justified: "Just as a nation, for its own safety, must know what other nations are up to, businessmen need information on what their competitors are doing. And with the competition growing daily more rugged, so is IE."

Obviously, the magazine has a point. Nor is all IE unethical or illegal. Only the poorest of businessmen would refuse to analyze trade magazine articles and published market data, avoid quizzing salesmen or suppliers, and in the merchandising fields, not send comparative shoppers to the competition. *Fortune* has declared that comparative shopping, while an example of business intelligence in acceptable form, can still be highly effective, "as in the case where Macy's, bound to observe manufacturers' minimum prices until it could prove others broke them, cracked the price-tag code of Masters, Inc., the giant New York discount house."

But with industry's research-and-development programs now exceeding $20 billion a year, with competition becoming increasingly keen and bitter as companies multiply and the market shrinks, many an industrialist or businessman acquires an amazingly flexible viewpoint as to what intelligence-gathering technique is acceptable.

Time has reported that nowhere is IE more virulent than in the oil industry. Our oil fields seem to be studded with almost as many spies as derricks. In one instance, the theft of some highly valuable geophysical maps started an investigation that uncovered an interesting bit of news: one of the company's most trusted employees was the silent partner of a small, competing oil company. Another case ended when an oil company employee was arrested while trying to sell some stolen exploration maps.

Detroit runs the oil industry a close second. Spies overrun the place. Security measures are fantastic. In many auto plants all locks are changed periodically. Code names are used to identify products and models. Important wastepaper is disposed of by means of drop slots, paper shredders and trash burners. When General Motors built its $175 million Technical Center, it equipped the plant with electronic devices that automatically drew the curtains over its studio windows at the approach of any aircraft. Despite all the precautions, auto spies today are peddling at least some details of cars destined for marketing two or three years hence.

The electronics industry is in equally bad shape. A Burns spokesman considers it one of the main targets for plain and fancy spy work. The president of a large West Coast electronics company says privately—and bitterly—that some of the new fringe electronic firms owe their existence to the secrets they stole.

Even the kiddie market is affected by IE. Appearing on a network television show, a leading New York toy manufacturer admitted the prevalence of espionage in his field. He stated that most of his employees are allowed to see only the portion of an intricate toy on which they are specifically working. The *Wall Street Journal* tells of the protective steps taken by the president of a Chicago toy design firm, whose employees must sometimes feel as though they are working on a top-secret defense project: "No toy designs go out for blueprinting and new toys are referred to by numbers, not names. Each night rough models and prototypes of toys under development are locked in the company vault. For six months a new employee works only on parts of toys; he is not told the purpose of the parts." Employees are not allowed to talk about their work on the toys, not even to their wives and children.

And things are so bad in the fashion industry that it has formed special committees whose sole object is the elimination of design piracy. At least one fashion industry spokesman has seen hypocrisy and futility in this move. Said Mr. Kenneth Collins in *Women's Wear Daily:* "Ninety percent of the trade lives by swiping styles. Everybody knows it. So why not cut out the pious fraud? Why go on forming trade groups and committees to fight sham battles which apparently no one wants to win? Lots of us are just as tired of this style morality as we once were of Prohibition."

Management Safeguards, a New York investigative firm, has found that the theft of confidential material is not always initiated by the firm that stands to gain by acquiring the information. Many times a malcontent, a person with a grudge against his own employer, will give secrets away to a man who formerly worked for the company and now owns his own competing firm.

The Harvard IE study notes that some companies hire an employee away from a competitor primarily for the brainpicking it can do. A number of firms, among them several chemical companies, try to protect themselves against this form of IE by insisting their key personnel sign secrecy agreements. When an ex-employee breaches such an agreement he leaves himself open to a lawsuit. Linde Air Products successfully sued a former worker who had been involved in the company's process for making synthetic star sapphires, then left to use the same process in his own company. Carter Products, Inc., won a suit against the Colgate-Palmolive Company after a Carter chemist who had signed a secrecy agreement went to work for Colgate-Palmolive and revealed the secret process involved in making Carter's Rise shaving cream. (Ulmont O. Cumming, who often works the other side of the street as a patent-infringement investigator, helped crack that one.)

The oldest—and still most reliable—method for stealing the other firm's trade secrets, however, is the one that proves itself so successful in snooping on employees: the use of undercover agents.

Ironically, the undercover agent does not always know that he is engaged in the business of snatching confidential data. A Washington, D. C., detective specializing in undercover work for the electronics field has told a *Fortune* writer about his routine. He gets his undercover men by placing want ads in the newspapers for the proper job category. The successful applicant is simply told that certain general information is needed from X Company; if the applicant can get on the payroll, the detective will boost his income by as much as $60 per week. The agent can expect bonuses, too, if he brings in particularly valuable morsels of information.

The detective's description of the indoctrination period, during which he breaks in a new man, is especially intriguing:

"I tell him how to write reports, what to look for, how to photograph documents, or get them out at night and bring them back in the morning. If the man is a technician, I interest him in being a detective someday and I pretend something quite different from what I'm actually trying to do. You gradually work him into what you are doing and tell him as little as possible. He doesn't know who your client is, or why you want the information, or which information is really important. That way, if he gets caught or outlives his usefulness, you have no trouble."

A case cited by the Harvard study shows how effective undercover market-data-snatching can be. A St. Louis camshaft manufacturer was consistently undersold by a Boston competitor even in the Missouri area. The St. Louis man determined to find out why. He hired a private detective, who in turn planted an undercover operative strategically inside the Boston plant. Within a month he knew how much the competition paid for its raw material, packaging costs, freight charges—practically everything but what the company officials were eating for dinner at night. Armed with the information, the St. Louis manufacturer was able to whittle down his costs and meet the competition. This may not be the best example of free enterprise at work, and it does nothing for the sorry state of privacy, but it sells camshafts.

Turnabout is fair play, and the private detective agencies that sell counterintelligence in the IE field, like Pinkerton's and Burns, also find undercover agents most effective. With undercover people making themselves so useful in so many ways, one cannot help wondering if they will not someday outnumber the legitimate employees in a given plant.

In a standard counter-IE operation, the undercover agent is planted inside the firm whose secrets are slipping away. But on occasion they are also planted in the company believed to be behind the spying. The Burns Agency did such a job for a company making highly specialized test panels used in the electronics industry. The panels were unique, were being manufactured by an ultrasecret process, and there was no competion—for a time. Suddenly the test panels manufacturer faced tremendous competition in the form of a new firm that not only offered similar test panels but underbid the originator on every job.

To clear up the mystery, Burns officials placed undercover people inside the victimized firm. Soon a strange pattern of fraternity became apparent. Eight of the firm's long-time employees—trusted men who held sensitive posts—kept themselves apart from the other workers. Consistently those eight lunched together, drank together, even lived in close proximity to each other.

Each of these eight men was shadowed. Now the bits and pieces of the investigation began to fit together. During lunchtime they were spotted taking things out to their cars. After work they often stopped in at a large building on the other side of town—a building that had as one of its tenants a small electronics firm.

Though it took some doing, Burns undercover agents were planted inside that small firm. The agents confirmed all the suspicions. The test panel originator's specifications, plans, blueprints and offers were finding their way to this competitor. The IE pipeline was clean and direct: the eight suspects actually *owned* the competing firm, though they had friends and relatives fronting for them. Lacking funds for research and for making up specifications, they simply based their entire operation on the purloined information.

The eight men were asked to resign from the firm they had been victimizing. Deprived of their only source of data, lacking the necessary capital or know-how to continue on their own, they soon folded their little enterprise.

Counterespionage can be as tricky as a counter move in chess. It can create situations that border on the ludicrous. Counterspies have been known to trail spies who were trailing the counterspies' clients. There is the memorable case of the private detectives who, while on an IE job, tried to sneak into a plant at night to lift some data—and were promptly arrested by plant guards working for their very own detective agency! Farce it may have been, but the plant owners were not amused. They filed a $60 million conspiracy suit.

Lawsuits, incidentally, are potentially the big hazard in IE. A firm may be successful in pirating the competition's secret methods, but in the process leaves itself open to legal retaliation. That retaliation can be massive—as when Lever Brothers launched a patent-infringement suit that cost Proctor & Gamble $5.6 million. Nevertheless, not all victimized companies are so eager to have their day in court. Lawsuits bring on publicity; publicity calls attention to what might have been slipshod security on the part of the complaining firm. Also, it can be extremely difficult for a company to prove that its secrets were stolen. Lawsuits are not as much of a deterrent, then, as they might be if they were more often used.

Lawsuits, no. More and more counterespionage activities, yes. In addition to undercover operations, these activities include all of the standard investigatory fare: shadowing, wiretapping, bugging. The *Wall Street Journal* tells of an Eastern steel forging company whose trade secrets were being leaked. The company hired an electronics expert to install wireless microphones in its offices. Several nights later, a private detective monitoring the transmitters heard the janitor phoning confidential data to a rival firm. He turned out to be no janitor at all. A metallurgical engineer employed by a rival firm, he had taken the janitor's job so he could have free access to desks and files at night.

The growing menace of IE has also led to the development of more sophisticated anti-intrusion devices. A New York firm has developed a new type of paper shredder that can digest some 500 lbs. of confidential letters, microfilm, ledger sheets, contracts or blueprints in an hour. The gadget sells for around $500. An indication of the prevalence of electronic eavesdropping in IE may be inferred by the ads that have appeared in the *Diner's Club Magazine*. A firm located in California offers an $89.75 "bug detector." The copy says that this contrivance "will detect wireless listening devices within eavesdropping range. Essential for anyone requiring top level security in conference room, home or office."

In 1959 the *Harvard Business Review,* a magazine for executives, conducted an IE poll. It aimed to learn to what extent industrial privacy is becoming industrial piracy. More than 1,500 executives were asked to choose between ethical and unethical techniques of gathering business information. Results of the survey indicated that "in nearly every case the younger executive is more likely to approve of a situation than an older executive."

A far greater percentage of the younger executives endorsed such practices as wining and dining a competitor simply to pump him; hiring a private detective to spy on a competitor's proving grounds; stealing a competitor's new model plans. For instance, nearly 30 percent of those under thirty-nine did not consider it immoral to hire a private investigator to spy on a competitor's proving grounds. Yet among executives over fifty, less than 10 percent approved.

The *Harvard Business Review* lamented that such differences in viewpoint "might well represent quite separate ethical standards on the part of younger and older executives." Will the younger executives retain their attitudes as they gain positions of increased responsibility and greater decision-making power? If so, the theft of business secrets will reach such proportions as to make today's encounters between industrial spies and counterspies seem a minor fracas—with privacy, both on a business and personal level, the major casualty.

10. The Electronic Invaders

"I eavesdrop for you
You eavesdrop for me,
We eavesdrop for each other!"
—Grammar school chant, as suggested
in the *Saturday Review,* July 15, 1950

THE WRITER OFFERING this suggestion, David L. Cohn, came by his flight of fancy as the result of a speech made at the 40th annual meeting of the Association of National Advertisers. The speaker, telling how hidden microphones and wire recorders were being used to eavesdrop on retail sales people, enthused, "With recording equipment concealed at the store counter . . . incompetence . . . in salespeople can be measured and a remedial program devised."

Remember, this was back in 1950 with the Goldfish Age just beginning to take form. The concept of workaday espionage was still in the realm of exotica. Mr. Cohn, waxing slightly less enthusiastic than the ANA speaker, took his *Saturday Review* readers with him on a satiric tour—a tour of life in which everybody is equipped with hidden microphones (jewel-encrusted ones for the ladies) and primary school kids lisp their grammar lesson as noted above.

Nearly 15 years have passed. Mr. Cohn's eavesdrop fancy has not thus far become reality. At least, there are as yet no mikes for the distaff side or indoctrination chants for the children. Unfortunately, this offers little room for rejoicing. The day of indiscriminate and universal eavesdropping looms ever closer. You have already observed some of the ways this electronic snooping is adapted to the business scene. That is only part of the story. A veritable horde of eavesdroppers operates both inside and outside government, both legally and illegally. Intelligence services, police departments, criminal elements and private investigators have joyously embraced the arts of bugging, wiretapping and related techniques.

While the laws controlling them have not kept pace, the techniques themselves have been undergoing considerable refinement. What *The Nation* a decade ago described as a "nightmare world in which no one can escape, even for a moment, the possibility that his every act and utterance are being officially observed" is practically here. Officially and unofficially, it is nearly impossible for you to avoid the electronic invaders if you are an eavesdropping target.

One important reason for this melancholy situation is the invention of the transistor and the printed circuit. These have allowed electronics manufacturers to effect an incredible miniaturization of their bugging equipment. A very popular (though expensive) gadget readily available today is the tiny wireless microphone attached to an equally small FM radio transmitter. Depending on the equipment, the transmitter can broadcast a distance of anywhere from one to five blocks. The signal is picked up by a receiving unit which demodulates it and feeds it to a tape recorder.

The wireless mike comes in a variety of disguises. Suppose an investigator wanted to record your conversation. He could do it with a miniature unit stuck casually in his shirt pocket; looking exactly like a king-size pack of cigarettes, it even has several filter tips showing. Or he could use a tiny wristwatch mike, the paraphernalia of comic strips come to life. Wireless mikes the size of a couple of lumps of sugar can be hidden in upholstery or secreted inside a bookshelf. They come installed in desk pen sets and picture frames. One manufacturer thoughtfully includes the picture of a church. These bugs operate on Liliputian batteries that last from 18 to 50 hours. If someone wanted to eavesdrop on you for much longer periods of time he could do that, too, needing only brief access to your premises. A type of bug that can be installed *inside* any wall socket draws its power from the building's electric current. These devices are available for $100 to $250 apiece.

A more sophisticated device performing even greater wonders is the latest thing in telephone bugs ($250). To use it the eavesdropper would need access to your telephones for a few minutes, just long enough to make the installation. This king of bugs listens in on both your side *and* the other side of your telephone conversation—*and* monitors all of the talk in the room when the phone is not in use. It is, investigators say, a great favorite with suspicious husbands who want to know what their wives are up to at home all day. Listening post for this device can be set up in an adjoining room or on floors above or below. In residential sections it also operates from across the street. Needing no batteries, it uses the current in the telephone line itself.

You cannot escape the determined eavesdropper even by going for a long ride in your car. There exists a wireless bug so constructed it can be clamped to the underside of a vehicle. It broadcasts to a transmitter in a surveillance car tailing at a distance of up to four city blocks.

Wired mikes have by no means gone out of business. The wire itself has undergone some startling changes, though. Hair wire so fine it can be varnished into the woodwork defies detection except with the aid of a magnifying glass. Also available is invisible conductive paint that actually takes the place of wire.

If the eavesdropper has access only to an outside or connecting wall of the room he wants to bug, he may use a spike mike. This $46.50 snooper's aid is exactly what it sounds like: a tiny mike attached to a 12-inch spike which is driven into the wall.

At the risk of punning, I should note that the miniature mike has a big brother. He comes in two varieties, both highly directional. The more familiar of these monsters is a parabolic mike equipped with a gigantic disk-shaped reflector that collects sound waves. The other is a huge tubular microphone aimed like a shotgun at the source of sound. Both can pick up whispers over 300 yards away and amplify them into intelligible words. Investigator Harvey Wolfe has described his use of the contraption: from a parked truck, he eavesdropped on two persons in a rowboat in the middle of a lake (in an industrial espionage case). Another detective overheard conversation in one office by aiming the device into its open window from another office at the same height but on the opposite side of the street.

It may well be a portent for the future that the parabolic mike has already been adapted for the kiddie market (or the fun-and-games crowd). Since 1962 you could buy an $18 version, "The Big Ear," in toy shops and some drugstores. "Pick up voices too distant for you to hear," coaxes the manufacturer. "Aim it at a group of friends a block away and hear every word."

Advances in the optical and photographic fields include tiny "spy" cameras (developed during the war and now popular with amateur photographers) and a 4 mm. movie camera —half the size of the smallest one currently on the market. Closed-circuit television has been miniaturized to the point that the camera "eye" can be hidden in a heating duct or light fixture. And the latest item in the still-camera field is a tiny *automatic* camera—activated by an ultrasonic signal— that utilizes infrared film to take photographs in total or near-total darkness.

Actually, we can only guess at the most sophisticated eavesdropping instruments currently available. Some are so hush-hush they are not even advertised. Solar Research, Inc., a Florida manufacturer of eavesdropping equipment, deliberately omits 45 of it products in its catalog. The *Wall Street Journal* quotes an official of Solar Research as saying that the Government requested the omissions.

Most manufacturers restrict their sales of bugging and wiretapping equipment to bona fide law enforcement agencies. This does not deter the private eavesdropper. If he is electronically-minded—and chances are that he is—he can fashion his own equipment at a fraction of the retail price. Otherwise he can buy it through *sub rosa* police contacts or purchase directly from mail order houses specializing in such items.

I have on my desk a catalog sent by just such a mail order house (located on the West Coast). It was not very difficult to get, In fact, all I had to do was clip an ad in a second-rate men's adventure magazine. The catalog came by return mail along with a small item which I had to buy in order to receive it.

A reassuring announcement at the front of the catalog states: "You don't need any permit, license or badge to order." Alongside the more virulent bugging equipment is a notice that cautions the buyer to "use it according to the laws of your community. However, these instruments may be used for amusement in your home, or at parties without violating any present laws."

Some of the items with which I can amuse myself at home: a correspondence course in bugging and wiretapping, a wiretap device, four different kinds of wireless mikes, FM receiving equipment. The latest fashions in the electronic eavesdropping field, home-delivered.

With so many intrusion devices now available, what of the future? Will the quest for ever more sophisticated instruments soon render privacy (from the standpoint of technology) totally obsolete? No question about that. As far back as 1955, eavesdropping expert Bernard Spindel told a Congressional investigating committee about a "sonic spectrum" which could "flood a room with a signal and obtain conversations without the need of concealing a mike or in fact ever entering or going near the room or building."

This raised a lot of eyebrows. Spindel, however refused to elaborate, saying, "I believe government agencies are now experimenting with this and it may be of a classified nature, so I will refrain from further comment about this in open session of the Committee."

At the time, *U.S. News & World Report* questioned a number of other experts about the "sonic spectrum." None knew what Spindel was talking about. Yet five years later surveillance systems using beams of micro- or ultrasonic waves had already been worked out. On May 26, 1960, Henry Cabot Lodge, then U.S. Ambassador to the United Nations, displayed a special reflector that had been removed from the Great Seal of the United States in the U.S. Embassy in Moscow. Little bigger than a half-dollar, this reflector had reportedly been planted by the Russians—who bounced a beam of microwaves off it, thus acquiring the ability to listen to every word of confidential conferences. Little data has been released on U.S. research in this highly classified field. Present equipment is said to be cumbersome, complex and costly. Five or ten years from now? Considering the rapidly advanc-

113

ing electronic eavesdropping technology, who knows but what even private specialists will be fooling around with light or sound waves.

Most frightening implication for the future is the notion of *built-in* surveillance—that is, surveillance systems built directly into new hotels, schools, jails, office buildings or other structures. In this Orwellian nightmare, the wiring could lead to a central listening and recording station.

No system of electronic eavesdropping is more inimical to privacy, none causes more gasps of horror from civil libertarians, and none gives greater point to the need for more stringent eavesdropping laws than the wiretap. Facile as the practice of bugging has become, wiretapping can be accomplished with equal ease. And it is being accomplished. On March 30, 1961, Senator Thomas J. Dodd announced on the Senate floor, "Each day in every major city of the nation, private telephone conversations are being listened to and recorded by unknown and unsuspected persons. . . . The full extent of telephone wiretapping cannot be known . . . but we do know from fragmentary evidence that this practice is shockingly widespread and that it is growing from year to year." This holds true even though tapping is not as blatant as it was during the early fifties. In that flamboyant era, private eavesdroppers took out classified telephone directory ads (mostly in California) advertising "electronic telephone monitoring." Public opinion precludes such arrogance these days. The tappers have scurried underground.

The all-encompassing nature of wiretapping is what makes it so horrifyingly destructive to privacy. The tap placed on one man's phone, to determine what he says in the context of one situation, catches dozens of irrelevant conversations—his own and other people's when they innocently use the same phone. When attorney Edward Bennett Williams represented Frank Costello in his denaturalization case in 1956, Williams discovered that evidence against his client had been obtained by wiretapping. Through a court order he obtained transcripts of all the wiretapped conversations and discovered just how pernicious the technique is. In his book *One Man's Freedom,* Williams described exactly what he found by going through the transcripts:

The transcripts included conversations between Costello and his wife, his doctor and his lawyer; conversations between Mrs. Costello and members of her family, her

114

doctor and her friends; conversations between one of the Costellos' maids and her husband, baring the most confidential and intimate family secrets.

Literally scores of persons who were suspected of no crime and who had committed no crime were subjected to this kind of surveillance. What they believed to be private conversations were invaded by the ears of the police. The most intimate details of the lives of these people became a matter of record in the files of the New York City police department as a result of this one wiretap.

The mere possibility that an eavesdropper might be listening has already caused some knowing people—I mean top-level businessmen, politicians and the like—to be more guarded, more wary when they use the phone. *Business Week* has quoted one New York executive as stating flatly, "I never say anything on the phone that I wouldn't want to be confronted with later."

Nor is a tap necessarily placed on a phone in order to develop a specific line of information. The tap may just be in the nature of a fishing expedition. The tapper who operated the Manhattan wiretap factory sometimes sampled telephone conversations hoping to catch something he could use as a selling point in approaching prospective clients. When he was later charged with putting a speculative tap on stripper Ann Corio's phone, she reportedly blurted, "I feel like I've been bathing in a glass bathtub."

What the American Civil Liberties Union calls wiretapping's "broad sweep" is demonstrated dramatically by the tapping of public telephones. And they *are* tapped, sometimes by private eavesdroppers, mainly by police officers working on a case. The ACLU gives some statistics for the period 1953–54. Of 3,588 phones legally tapped by New York City police during that period, 1,617—nearly half—were public telephones. By the nature of wiretapping machinery not only the suspect's conversations—but the remarks of *everyone* who uses the tapped phone—are monitored. Columbia University's Professor Alan F. Westin has offered a striking example of what the wiretapping net can haul in when it is used on a public phone.

"In the course of tapping a single telephone," explained Dr. Westin in the *Columbia Law Journal*, "a police agent recorded conversations involving at the other end, the Julliard School of Music, Brooklyn Law School, Consolidated Radio Artists, Western Union, Mercantile National Bank, several restaurants, a drugstore, a real estate company, many lawyers, a stationery store, a dry cleaner, numerous bars, a garage, the Prudential Insurance Company, a health club, the Medical Bureau to Aid Spanish Democracy, dentists, brokers, engineers, and a New York Police Station."

Despite the sorry wonders it leaves us to behold, there is nothing complicated about wiretapping technique. Its concepts are easily understood by anyone with a little electronic or communications engineering knowledge. Indeed, *The Eavesdroppers* devotes 24 pages to a detailed explanation of the wiretapping art in laymanese, complete with diagrams. Essentially, the wiretapper either hooks up a wire to the telephone line to be tapped or places an induction coil in close proximity to the line. Listening in on earphones he can —most often does—tape the conversation. (One new $995 device not only records conversations, it also prints the number, time and date of each call.)

Legal taps (in permissive states) are made *only* by bona fide law enforcement officers who apply for a court order much as they do for a search warrant. The court order is then presented to the telephone company, which formally releases the necessary line information. Judges, being human, vary in their responses to requests for wiretap orders. Some grant them readily, without much regard for the victims' privacy, others are hard-nosed about it. It may be safely assumed that police officers, also being human, keep track of judges' attitudes and rely most on the easygoing ones.

The trick to *illegal* wiretapping lies in spotting the correct line, the line to be tapped, either at the terminal box or at some other convenient point. Since each telephone line is strung with dozens of others, this takes some doing. It is done best by getting the telephone company to help—in other words, to provide the same line information it does in the case of legal taps.

Now, the telephone companies do not distribute this data indiscriminately. Most take reasonable security precautions to see that data such as pair-and-cable numbers do not fall into the wrong hands. But reasonable is hardly akin to total; as testimony before the 1959 Senate wiretap hearings brought out, there is plenty of margin for leaks. Tappers working illegally may use paid informants—telephone company employees—who have access to the information; the tappers themselves may be ex-phone company employees who know just how to call in for the data (which is legitimately used by linemen on the job); sometimes, too, a private tapper works closely with a police officer who has access to the information on the q.t.

Once he has the line information in hand, the wiretapper still has to go out and make the actual tap. Amazingly, this often proves to be the easiest part of the job. You might take it for granted the tap is made in the dead of night by sneaking, skulking, furtive figures operating nervously in the shadows. Nothing could be further from the truth. The wiretapping fraternity employs few stealthy methods. Samuel Dash held Senators at the wiretap hearing spellbound with his masterful description of how the illegal tappers operate:

"Your private specialist who taps . . . does it in the open and right in front of your eyes. In this country we are bedeviled by people who come to homes and check meters and car repair people, telephone company people, who legitimately have a right to check our lines—the private specialist fits himself right into that American picture. He has usually a green telephone company truck which he has bought used. Almost every one of them has it. He usually bedecks himself with screwdrivers and pliers and has wire hanging all over him, the more the better. He will walk right up to a home and ring the doorbell and say, 'Madam, I am from the telephone company; your line has been reported, trouble on the line.'

"The dear lady usually opens the door, shows him the telephone, and sometimes lends him a screwdriver, if he needs it.

"We have one case where a wiretapper walked into a restaurant and told the owner that the telephone booth there was out of order and he had to repair it. The restaurant owner pushed back tables, made people leave to eat in another place in the restaurant, stood and watched him while he installed a wiretap and thanked him for his services as he left.

"Wiretappers have worked on the top of poles in the presence of police and supervisors of the telephone company. One time a supervisor commented, 'They have got you working up there pretty late.'

"His answer was, 'Yes, it is a tough job.' The supervisor replied, 'Well, don't work too hard,' and departed. Take the lawyers' offices, professional people's offices, any big office building—they have maintenance men who go in and out of the offices and I have been able to observe the telephone multiple box of a large office open and a man standing on the ladder working on it and no one questioning as to whether he was a maintenance man and had a right to be there.

"They have walked in, as I said, to any office or any place and in the presence of the person who is being tapped installed the tap in the guise of a repairman. I think that this is quite noteworthy and might lead people to do a little more questioning as to the authenticity of a man who comes to their home."

The telephone companies are not happy about this. They are caught squarely in the middle. They want John Q. Public to make increasing use of the telephone. But if John Q. gets the notion that somebody might secretly be listening in, he will make fewer calls than before. The phone company would lose money. Thus we may safely believe Mr. Wellington Powell, a New York Telephone Company executive, who made the following policy statement on behalf of his company: "We do not like any invasion of the privacy of communications by wiretapping and we welcome federal and state laws which strengthen this privacy and reduce the opportunities and temptations to invade the privacy of the telephone user."

Nevertheless, some experts feel that the phone companies are not doing enough to eliminate illegal wiretapping. Samuel Dash has charged that the companies have not effected adequate controls, have failed to cooperate fully with the police in finding or prosecuting wiretappers, and have not developed new apparatus to deal with the problem. Kings County, New York, District Attorney Edward S. Silver has declared that the telephone companies should report all wiretapping cases, though they might prefer not to "because they don't want to give the impression that perhaps the telephone isn't quite as private as it might be."

A spokesman for the American Telephone and Telegraph Company insists that telephone companies belonging to the Bell System follow stringent security measures within their own offices. Also, he said, employees are exhorted on the theme of "secrecy of communications," and made fully cognizant of state and federal laws dealing with the subject. Violators are immediately fired. The spokesman added that the Bell System's laboratories are "always working on methods to improve telephone privacy." But he admitted that "at the present time there is no device or gadget that can be obtained which would guarantee absolute protection from electronic eavesdropping or wiretapping."

Exactly what happens when a Bell System subscriber reports that he thinks his phone is being tapped? According to the AT & T spokesman, the complaint is immediately investigated. A three-way physical check of the subscriber's circuit covers the central office, along the line from the central office to the subscriber's terminal, and the station equipment. The subscriber is informed when the results are negative. If some "unexplained or suspicious" condition is found, the appropriate law enforcement agency is notified "and the matter is turned over to that office for further investigation, including any necessary contact with the complaining subscriber."

Few complaints are received. But then, as the telephone companies are well aware, few subscribers know it when their phones are being tapped.

Illegal wiretapping is not restricted to private specialists working for their private clients. Investigations conducted over the past two decades by newspapers, state committees and the Senate hearing have uncovered the existence of widespread illegal tapping by local law enforcement agencies. In his testimony, Dash summed up the disheartening situation:

"Every major city we looked at, illegal wiretapping was practiced. It was done on the theory that the community needed the protection, the law enforcement officer was given the job of doing the protecting and the people didn't know what was good for them."

This arrogant approach to the law cannot help but breed further contempt for it. It is hardly surprising that Dash offered testimony to suggest instances of collusion between private tappers and police officers. He also said that some police wiretapping (in bookmaking cases) has been effected solely for the purpose of "locating the bookie to get on the payroll rather than to make a law enforcement arrest."

So much for local law enforcement. Electronic eavesdroppers are busily at work in our nation's capital, too. While the Pennsylvania Bar Association Endowment study did not include tapping and bugging on a federal level, reports out of Washington leave no doubt about the situation there. Newsman Ben H. Bagdikian, on the Washington scene for a number of years, stated in a *Saturday Evening Post* article on news managing that a considerable number of Pentagon officials take it for granted their offices are bugged. And "almost every defense correspondent I talked to," he added, "assumed his telephone, office and home are tapped by some government agency."

In mid-1963 I had occasion to call, from my New York

home, a reporter stationed in Washington. As our conversation drew to a close he said, quite unexpectedly, "You ought to look into wiretapping here, too. I know my phone's been tapped but I don't give a damn." He implied that he never says anything over the phone that smacks the least bit of controversy.

Telephone monitoring is not always synonymous with wiretapping, of course. It may simply mean that one of the two parties to the call is secretly recording the conversation or having a secretary make notes unbeknownst to the party at the other end. It may also mean that a third party is surreptitiously listening in on an extension. This insidious form of home-grown eavesdropping goes on extensively in private offices. Sometimes news of its presence comes as a shock. When I told a magazine editor with whom I had been doing business for years that I was working on a book about privacy, he whispered, "You ought to write about my boss. He's got the habit of listening in on the staff's phone calls—without announcing himself."

Telephone monitoring is an established practice is government offices, too. So prevalent is it in Washington, in fact, that both in 1961 and 1962 the House Government Information subcommittee probed its extent. In 1961 the subcommittee found 33 federal agencies practicing some form of telephone monitoring. The 1962 probe showed a little improvement, but plenty of room for more. Fifteen federal agencies required the party at the other end of the line to be notified only if a verbatim account of the conversation was being made—which meant secretaries could still listen in secretly to jot down names, dates and references. Understandably, the subcommittee wondered just where jotting ends and full-scale eavesdropping begins. Nine agencies (including the CIA and the Department of Justice) had no inhibiting regulations at all—monitoring could occur at will. Favorite gadgets used for such eavesdropping are transmitter cutoffs—more appropriately called "snooper buttons" by knowledgeable Washington secretaries. These devices permit one person in the same office to listen in on another person's call without breathing or background noises being transmitted over the snooper's phone. There were 4,790 of them reported in use, each of them costing the American taxpayer 25¢ per month in rental fees.

Looking over the results of its first probe, the subcommittee allowed that there were indications of "a dangerous drift toward a huge bureaucracy peering over the shoulder of the citizen." And in its second report the subcommittee strongly urged regulations which would "clearly specify that advance notice must be given whenever a secretary or any other person or recording device is placed on the line for any purpose whatsoever."

Good advice, it would seem, for private firms as well as for government agencies.

Apt to horrify any reasonable person are the federal and state laws covering electronic eavesdropping. As Attorney General Robert F. Kennedy has so accurately put it, the situation is "legal chaos."

At the crux of the confusion lie an ambiguously worded statute and some equally fuzzy Supreme Court decisions. The statute is in Section 605 of the Federal Communications Act of 1934, whose pertinent, troublesome portion reads as follows: ". . . no person not being authorized by the sender shall intercept any communication and divulge or publish the existence, contents, substance, purport, effect or meaning of such intercepted communication to any person. . . ."

Now, like truth itself, these words seem to shift their shape and meaning depending on the eyes that take them in. A substantial number of legal experts—albeit those with a strong bent for affirming civil liberties—have held that this means a flat-out, no-compromise wiretapping ban applying both to private and law enforcement eavesdroppers. The Justice Department (wiretapping through the FBI) has chosen to see things quite a bit differently. It has, through a succession of Attorney Generals, maintained that the ban covers only interception *and* divulgence. In other words, interception is legal just so long as the information is kept within the police agency and not used as evidence in court. Many states, too, formulated their own wiretap laws with little regard for the total ban implied by Section 605.

The various U.S. Supreme Court decisions handed down since the birth of the puzzling, controversial statute have not exactly fitted together all the pieces of the puzzle. In 1937 the Court held that Section 605 applied to federal law enforcement officers and rendered wiretap evidence inadmissible in federal courts. In another decision, it held that evidence from leads acquired by wiretapping was not admissible. It also decided that Section 605 was applicable to both interstate and intrastate telephone calls.

Subsequently, the Court held that listening in on one end of the telephone conversation is not an interception in terms of Section 605. It has held that only the parties to a conver-

121

sation could object to the use of wiretap evidence in court. It has held that the police can listen in on an extension telephone if one of the parties to the conversation agrees to it. The Court has decided that wiretapping by state officials violates Section 605—*but* that the evidence, though illegally obtained, may be used in state courts if the state so permits. And it has held that federal courts cannot prevent wiretap evidence from being used in state trials, though the evidence was illegally obtained. But state law enforcement officials are increasingly reluctant to present such evidence because they have broken a federal law in obtaining it.

On a state level there is an equal amount of confusion and contradiction. By now 33 states (among them Illinois, Michigan, Pennsylvania, Florida and California) have instituted total wiretap bans that apply to police officials as well as to private tappers. Six states (including New York) have created partial bans—allowing law enforcement officers to tap pursuant to court orders, forbidding private tappers to operate under any conditions, In a few states a private individual may tap his own line.

All this refers to the wiretap alone. We must not forget all those other intricate little electronic eavesdropping devices, for the confusion extends to them as well. Some states (New York, for instance) outlaw the use of *any* electronic eavesdropping device by private individuals. Other states prohibit wiretapping but do permit private investigators to install bugs. In a few states the statutes are so ambiguous that law courts might hold the bugging of a room to be illegal, but the use of a parabolic mike in a public place to be no violation.

The trouble with even the best statute is that its effectiveness is in direct ratio to its enforcement. Nowhere is this more evident than the wiretap bans. Though wiretapping is construed to be a federal crime, federal law enforcement officers tap. Because they tap, they cannot very well prosecute state and city law enforcement officers for doing the same thing. Because state and city police officers do tap, they cannot prosecute private wiretappers—at least with any real vigor. Nor can the Federal Government. From 1952 to 1961 there were only 14 federal prosecutions for wiretapping. In the past 15 years there have been only a handful of prosecutions in New York. Though wiretapping has been a penal offense in California for 5 decades, there were less than half-a-dozen prosecutions from 1939 to 1959.

In 1962 Attorney General Kennedy strove to clear the wiretap air. He proposed sweeping new legislation (still under examination by the Senate Judiciary Committee) that would legitimize official wiretapping under strict conditions and rigorous safeguards. Not surprisingly, the FBI would be granted power to wiretap and to present wiretap recordings as evidence in national security and "high crime" cases. State law enforcement officials would also be permitted to wiretap—and to present evidence—solely in cases of murder, kidnapping and "organized" crime, pursuant to court orders. All other wiretapping, both official and private, would be prohibited. Fairly heavy penalties would be meted out to violators.

Challenging this and any other bill that would legitimize electronic eavesdropping is the American Civil Liberties Union. Even if permitted under limited circumstances, the ACLU insists, wiretapping "would seriously impair the privacy so necessary to a free society" and is in violation of "the fundamental rights protected by the Fourth Amendment to the Constitution." To make the practice lawful would be to move the nation "closer toward a police state where constant government intrusion and surveillance inhibit and constrict a free people."

Moving from principle to practicality, the ACLU points out that the actual need for wiretapping has not been demonstrated, since 33 states have outlawed it entirely and several district attorneys from populous areas have testified against its use. Energetic investigative work, the civil liberties organization suggests, obviates the need for wiretapping. And it points to the ease with which the "fruits" of electronic eavesdropping—the tapes derived from it—can be doctored.

Technologically, it is possible to alter completely the sense and meaning of what has been caught on tape—with no way for even an expert technician to detect the alteration. To start with an extremely simple example. Suppose you have said, in a statement recorded on tape, "I love the United States and hate anything having to do with Communism." It is child's play to erase a few words, retape the result to produce an intact tape in which you say, "I love Communism." Words can be erased, spliced, placed in completely different positions. Even more astounding—and frightening: syllables within a word can be lifted out and put elsewhere to build a completely new word said in your voice but not in the original statement at all. The Subcommittee on Constitutional Rights was told of one experiment in which a speech in favor of God, for motherhood and against Communism was changed within two hours to one admitting the theft of

123

money, advocating the overthrow of the Government, and confessing to the murder of an FBI agent. Not even an electronics expert could tell the altered tape from the original one, though electronic equipment was used in the attempt.

Needless to say, the ease with which a person's words can be altered to produce the exact opposite of what he really said makes electronic spying even more dangerous in the hands of private eavesdroppers who already break the law and might be willing to go much further for a dollar. The ethics of the profession is at best dubious, not only because it has specialized in an illegal area but because there have been many instances in which the eavesdroppers double-crossed their own clients. In some cases they have done so by insisting on more money before turning over the tapes, if they deemed the information valuable enough. In other cases the eavesdroppers sold their services both to the original clients and to the subjects who were supposedly under secret surveillance. Altering tapes is something countenanced by the same type of mentality.

Even among those authorities championing limited use of wiretapping by law enforcement agencies, it is difficult—if not impossible—to find one willing to extend the right to tap to private parties. All suggestions from lawyers and police officials, all proposed bills, incorporate a total ban on private eavesdropping and provide for stiff penalties in cases where the law is flouted. Penalties that, presumably, would be backed up by strict enforcement of the regulations.

Is that enough to curb the electronic eavesdroppers? Experience would indicate that it is not enough. Even in total-ban states, and even when there has been an occasional prosecution for illegal tapping, the practice continues. No law that provides punishment solely for the eavesdropper gets to the heart of the problem, not so long as there is a continuing demand for his services by people well able to pay for them.

What must be dealt with, I think, is not only the instrument of intrusion and its technicians, but the client whose arrogant philosophy holds that a man's privacy is totally unworthy of respect. One way of handling this situation might be to impose sanctions not just on the eavesdropper but on his client, as well. If punishment in electronic eavesdropping cases could be extended to the person who orders the job— then the demand might well drop in a hurry.

Until that happens, it will be difficult to avoid or outwit a determined electronic eavesdropper. However, if you wish to take the trouble, you can ensure yourself a really private, eavesdrop-proof conversation. These are the measures currently available to anyone bent on foiling the electronic invaders of privacy:

You can hire an anti-intrusion specialist to check your premises for bugs. Some of the private detective agencies offer the service. A few electronic firms specialize in the detection of hidden listening devices. One actually advertises its services in the classified section of the Manhattan telephone directory.

You can circumvent wiretapping by having a phone installed directly behind a neon sign. The sign acts like a transformer. What the wiretapper will wind up with is nothing more than a roar on his recorder.

You can, if money is no object, build a completely eavesdrop-proof room. First, make sure to have very heavy doors and walls, to prevent sound and vibrations from leaking out of the room. Second, use plenty of sound-absorbing materials on the ceiling. Third, completely enclose the premises with a metal shielding so no radio or microwaves will be able to enter or leave. Fourth, make sure to use heavy curtains or blinds over the windows, rendering them opaque to light beams. Fifth, hire an electrical engineer to fix up the lighting circuits so they cannot carry radio waves. Sixth, hire an anti-intrusion expert to detect and jam FM channels. Seventh, keep your voice low when talking to someone in the room; it also helps to move around, speak in code, and let water run for background noise. Finally, never use the telephone—or, if you must use it, have the electrical engineer fix you up with a device that carries the speech signal underground.

All this may sound like a lot of bother. But if you want to make absolutely sure of your privacy of conversation these days, you have to work for it.

Intrusion in the Community

11. Three Community Pressures

> *Soundproofing is the only technological contribution I can think of that has been an aid to the right to be let alone.*
> —RICHARD H. ROVERE, *in the Autumn 1958 issue of* The American Scholar

NOT ONLY HAVE science and technology virtually excluded the state of privacy from their beneficences (paper shredders and bug locators hardly seem a windfall), but all of the inventions in the field of intrusion seem to be snapped up with nary a glimmer of reflection about the morality of their use. Though there are still plenty of people in business and elsewhere who reject employing bugs, wiretaps, lie detectors and the like, the trend appears to say, "If it works, let's use it—and the hell with the consequences!"

In this chapter we will take a cursory look at three things that loom large in our everyday lives—the telephone, advertising, and the press—to see how they have been affected by the trend in recent years. The purpose is not so much to criticize certain practices as to show how attitudes toward privacy are being crystallized in our communities.

It goes without saying that no invention, not even the doorbell or the mailbox, is as effective as the telephone in penetrating the inner recesses of our homes. Consequently, the telephone is coming into increasing favor as a selling instrument. The salesman who rings the doorbell may be ignored; the advertising circular that comes through the mails may be tossed unopened into the wastebasket; but it takes an iron constitution and a will made of unearthly stuff to disregard the persistent ringing of the telephone. To show the compelling power of the phone, writer John Keats has told the story of a suicide-bent man perched fourteen stories high on the ledge of a New York hotel room, who, when the phone began to ring, climbed unthinkingly back into his room to answer it. As an illustration of the way this power is coming to be increasingly turned into a selling and advertising tool, *The New York Times* described the workings of a vast telephone network—Eugene Gilbert's Consumer Opinion Institute. The firm employs some 10,000 part-time telephone interviewers. These people perform a dual role, functioning both as pollsters and telephone advertisers (though they do not mix the roles). In 1959 Consumer Opinion Institute placed 1,000,000 calls on behalf of its clients. In 1962 the company placed about 5,000,000 calls. In 1963 it was expected to place nearly 10,000,000 calls.

Consumer Opinion Institute is just one organization in the business of placing calls. There are hundreds of other telephone marketing outfits, large and small, across the nation. The boom in business sales calls is giving them more work, too. We can easily accept as an understatement the *Times'* conclusion that the situation "means more business calls for the average consumer."

Now, it may be safely assumed that this turn of events is a source of great joy and comfort to the telephone industry. It may also be assumed that a percentage of the population is delighted to receive unexpected telephone calls offering cut-rate magazine subscriptions or a quiz that will net the answerer five free dance lessons. However, one suspects there is in this country a substantial body of telephone subscribers for whom such calls are more of a disturbance than an opportunity. And the question that comes to mind is: has the telephone industry extended its concern for the privacy of communications to include unwanted and unsolicited business calls?

The answer—for at least two reasons—appears to be in the negative. The first reason concerns a fairly new Bell Telephone invention. This is an electronic device that records a sales spiel, selects the numbers to call, calls them, and delivers the pitch—all automatically. The subscriber does not even have a chance to hang up on a human being, should he be so inclined. When *Advertising Age* columnist E. B. Weiss picked up his ringing telephone and discovered he was listening to an "electronic selling monster" (his words), he became so infuriated that he wrote the Bell System an open letter in his column. Praising the organization for having been one of the true leaders in image building, Weiss suggested in no uncertain terms that in this case it may have begun to overlook its human relations.

The second reason the telephone industry seems unconcerned about privacy outside the realm of wiretapping is its negative attitude toward those folk who would prefer not to have their telephone numbers listed. And, understandably enough, there are more such people around than ever before. According to the *Wall Street Journal*, about 14 percent of the 2.1 million Illinois Bell Telephone Co. phones in the Chicago area are unlisted. More than 8 percent of New York Telephone Co. subscribers have unlisted phones. The California Water & Telephone Co., which services the suburbs of Los Angeles, reported 13 percent unlisted numbers. Five years ago that figure was 8 percent.

The telephone companies are dismayed by what has happened. They want no part of unlisted numbers and are doing their best to discourage people from asking for them. Privacy? They refuse to accept that as the reason for the growing popularity of unlisted numbers, and shrug off the trend as indicating little more than a desire for a new kind of status symbol. Their thinking is reflected in this statement from an Independent Telephone Association official: "It's like belonging to an exclusive club. People hear about important persons having unlisted numbers, so they think if their numbers are unlisted it will make other people think they are important." This may come as big news to some subscribers who thought they merely wanted to be left alone. Privacy-seeking subscribers are often even more surprised when the telephone company penalizes them by charging extra for unlisted numbers, as some companies do.* The telephone industry, it seems, is making privacy not only harder to come by but more expensive.

* Phone companies say unlisted numbers cost them money—because of the time it takes the information operator to determine that the number is not listed. Other reasons why they are against the idea; subscribers might not be reached in case of emergencies; people who want an unlisted number and cannot get it go away mad.

Turning to advertising, we could reflect that it is in all its aspects an intrusive force in our lives. So it is; but to give the thought serious consideration would be to dismiss both advertising's important function in educating us to new products and to negate also the many creative ads that are a pleasure to view for their own sake. As for the objectionable forms of advertising that might be considered invasions of privacy—well, we are not exactly powerless if we do not want to be. Hard-sell ads can be ignored; offensively blaring TV commercials can be turned down or—better yet—off; ugly billboards despoiling the countryside would not be there if a protesting public let its state legislators and the sponsoring companies know exactly how it felt.

However, for the past decade or so the advertising industry—through market and motivational researchers—has displayed an increasing tendency to use disguised psychological tests, electronic snooping instruments, gumshoe tactics and optical spies of its own devising to find out just how people react to products, labels, packages, ads, displays and slogans. Whether the data obtained is used to manipulate the consumer on an unconscious level, as Vance Packard's *The Hidden Persuaders* revealed, or whether it is used to appraise and create straightforward ads, the fact is that much of what is going on smacks of Peeping-Tomism. The research end of the advertising field likes to say that it has adopted the techniques of social science. Indeed, many sociologists, psychologists, and anthropologists have abandoned the cloistered academic halls for the plush carpeting in Madison Avenue's offices. But while social scientists working on scientific projects disagree within their own fraternity as to the ethical limits of their secret intrusions, the market researchers seem to have been much less prone to this kind of introspection. At least some of the sleuthing methods that have become common practice would so indicate.

These days the housewife shopping in a supermarket may well be filmed by a hidden movie camera while she gives her rapt attention to a new display or a new product. The camera eye might observe her facial expressions, gestures, the length of time it takes her to make her selection—what in the trade is called the "physical dimension of brand selection"— as she studies the product. Or the camera might be built right into the counter to record secretly her eye-blink rate. The rate at which a person blinks his eyes gives an indication of his inner tension; in a shopper, it reveals a great deal about the impact a particular display makes on her.

The practice of installing hidden movie cameras began with a few test markets in a few test cities. Now the game is played nationally and hundreds of supermarkets are taking part in places like Columbus, Ohio, and Indianapolis, Indiana, to name just two. The ad agency involved makes a straight cash deal with the supermarket chain or, more often, with the manager of the individual market in which the camera is to be hidden. One city could easily have several camera-equipped markets, each shooting away for a different research group.

Do supermarkets ever refuse to go along? Few, it appears. Most are glad to cooperate. A notable exception is the A & P chain, which does not permit the installation of hidden cameras in its markets. When I queried an A & P marketing representative about this, he told me that the chain does its own market research but confirmed the ban on hidden cameras. "No ethical considerations are involved," he explained. "We simply see no necessity for it."

However, outside market researchers have not been fazed by the chain's refusal to cooperate. When they want to find out what shopper reaction to a certain product is in an A & P market, they merely send one of their number to mingle incognito with the crowd. Unable to film, he simply watches the shoppers to see how they are reacting. As for what is being said by the ladies as they talk to each other or to the clerks—with a miniature tape recorder hidden inside his clothes, he records it all. Researchers "wired for sound" may also go into markets other than A & P to record what is being said.

Hidden movie cameras serve other purposes as well. *Consumer Reports* told of a hidden camera test conducted by the National Association of Transport Advertising. A king-sized advertising poster was mounted on the outside of a bus in Philadelphia. Purpose of the test was to find out how many people of either sex looked at the poster with one or with both eyes. The specially designed robot cameras were mounted inside the bus, camera lenses pointed toward the people on the street. Controlled electronically, the cameras systematically took pictures of all eyes turned on the ad "during 10-second periods, every 10 minutes during all daylight hours for 30 consecutive days."

Hidden microphones are also helpful in testing customer reaction. They have found particular favor at trade fairs and manufacturers' shows. Secreted in display booths, they lead

130

to recording equipment that captures (for later analysis) what the visitors are saying about the products on display.

Two-way mirrors are occasionally used to observe customer reaction in stores and have found great favor within some of the motivational research laboratories, where they are used in studies with participating consumer volunteers. *Business Week* has described one such study conducted by the Opinion Research Corp. Researchers secretly peered through two-way mirrors while the male volunteers inspected sports jackets on a rack. The idea was to find out how customers approach that kind of a potential purchase—whether they first look at the tags, or feel the material, or check the weight of the coat.

The unmistakable conclusion to be derived from all of this is that the consumer's privacy is a nonexistent factor in the creation of research techniques that gather data for more effective advertising. Some paragraphs back, the alliance between marketing research and social science was established. There are universally-sponsored sociologists, too, who use bugs, hidden cameras, two-way mirrors and similar devices in their study of man and society. But there are many other social scientists, like Professor Edward Shils of the University of Chicago, who condemn such use even for legitimate scientific projects.

Writing in *The Human Meaning of the Social Sciences,* Professor Shils stated:

> The development of new mechanical devices for observation, such as small soundless motion picture cameras, small unnoticeable microphones, and other undiscernible sound-recording equipment, has precipitated a very urgent issue, and one on which social scientists should take an unequivocal position. They cannot, on any grounds, approve observations of private behavior, however technically feasible, *without the explicit and fully informed permission of the person to be observed.* (Italics mine.)

Less virulent than some of the other techniques, but worthy of note if only for the intriguing uses to which closed-circuit television is being put these days, are the focused group interviews conducted by the Fuller, Smith & Ross Agency. When a merchandising problem calls for interviews, about 25 volunteer consumers, usually women, are brought into the agency. They are not told about the problem; they believe they are there to "help test a television commercial." Only about seven or eight women are actually chosen to participate in the group discussion, which remains completely spontaneous and unstructured. A discussion leader casually steers the conversation into areas of interest to the client. These often include reaction to his products. The ladies realize they are being televised because the leader makes no secret about wearing the kind of headset usually associated with TV. What the ladies do not know is that the client and agency people are watching the proceedings over receiving sets located elsewhere in the building. Nor do they realize that the client may be asking questions right along, communicating with the discussion leader through the headset. When the group interview is over, the women are asked to sign releases covering their voices and ideas.

Even children are being watched covertly for marketing purposes. Tully Plesser, director of marketing at Fuller, Smith & Ross, is in charge of a new "creative drama" technique. Children whose ages range from six to ten are brought in by an outside recruiting firm to talk, ask questions or play-act in situations about products in the kiddie market. The children have been carefully chosen as to age, sex, family income and other characteristics. The only adult present during the creative drama session is Carole Schwartz, a creative drama teacher and producer of children's TV programs. But the ad agency people are there in spirit nonetheless, via their receiving sets and Miss Schwartz's headset.

The right of privacy meets a powerful adversary in the right of the press to exercise its functions without undue restraints. At its best—and there is fortunately a lot of the best—the American press is nosy in the finest sense: not only in presenting and clarifying events, but also in exposing corruption and injustice, and helping to bring about needed social reforms. Most of us would not have it be less nosy in this sense. We agree with Tocqueville's observation, made a century ago, that "in order to enjoy the inestimable benefits which liberty of the press insures, it is necessary to submit to the inevitable evils which it engenders."

However, submission does not necessarily mean total surrender; though publishers and editors are sometimes prone to wrap themselves around the American flag and proclaim loudly their freedom to present the news, the fact remains that they are also in business to make money. And much of what passes for news is more properly gossip or the exploitation of personal misery. In cases such as these the individual has the right—even the duty—to stand up for his privacy and, if necessary, seek protection for it. As Professor Zelermyer puts it, "The Constitutional guarantee of a free press must not be allowed to serve as a cloak of protection against liability for unwarranted exploitations of privacy."

Indeed, it was the excesses of the press that were in the first place responsible for putting privacy as a legal right in the American lawbooks. Samuel Warren, co-author with Louis Brandeis of "The Right to Privacy," was a prominent Boston socialite who found himself in the public eye with a vengeance when he got married. The Boston papers, and in particular a tabloid called *Saturday Evening Gazette,* reported the couple's activities in lurid detail. Other Boston bluebloods had received the same kind of treatment and simply took it as best they could. Not Warren. He got together with his former law partner, Brandeis, and after mulling over the subject of privacy in all its ramifications for a few years they came out with their epoch-making *Harvard Law Review* article promulgating a legal right to privacy.

If an individual in Brandeis and Warren's day needed the protection of law against an excessively prying press, he needs it more so today. We are in a time when few subjects are taboo; newspapers and magazines can delve into many more areas of a person's private life without offending popular taste than was possible in the past. We live in an age in which public curiosity has few restraints; as Milton R. Konvitz pointed out in *Fundamental Liberties of a Free People,* "almost everything has become newsworthy; and the 'candid camera' is everywhere." Thus we see spread broadside in our newspapers the suffering face of an accident victim who was obviously in no condition to give or refuse permission to have his photo taken. We read all the juicy little tidbits that occurred in the lives of a once-anonymous couple now grown "newsworthy" by reason of a messy divorce. In rape cases we are given not only a news account but the victim's identity and address as well (though in a few states identification is prohibited). Personal sorrow is turned into a public circus as we read not only the pertinent facts relating to a victim of misfortune, but irrelevancies about his wife, children and parents. We read about a forthcoming trial, particularly if it might prove sensational, in such minute detail that the fairness of the trial itself is at times impaired—not only because of what is revealed but also because of the slant the paper has taken.

Finally, we need to be protected against the dangers of

133

press intrusion more than ever now because the inventions of intrusion that have benefited business, labor, advertising and other groups can hardly be expected to have been overlooked by the press. Nor have they. Pocket-size tape and wire recorders either carried in a shoulder holster or elsewhere secreted on the body are standard equipment with many newspaper reporters. Miniature "spy" cameras and high-powered telephoto lenses, unheard of at the time Warren expressed his anger toward the press, are available to every newspaper office today. Some papers monitor all calls that come into the office. Bugging is resorted to at times; *The Eavesdroppers* tells how one New York paper managed to be first on the street with details of the Rosenberg executions by hiding a tiny microphone-transmitter inside the coat collar of its reporter on the scene.

When it comes to concentration on the most sordid kind of gossip and the revelation of the most private acts, certainly no publication in the history of American journalism has ever surpassed that Goldfish Age product, the magazine called *Confidential*. In its heyday during the early and middle 1950's (the title was subsequently sold and the magazine is presently published by another organization), *Confidential* adopted nearly every intrusive technique imaginable in its unremitting effort to invade the privacy of Hollywood stars and other celebrities. It paid several private detectives five-figure retainers to drag out the dirty wash that would subsequently be exposed or hinted at within its pages. One of its gumshoes later told of hiding in the bushes one day to film the activities of a famous actress and her fiancé. It authorized the tapping of telephones and the extensive use of bugging equipment. It had paid informers and undercover agents on tap; one was a brothel madam, and when California finally indicted *Confidential* on a criminal libel charge in 1957, the madam testified she had been asked to wear a wristwatch microphone and a miniature tape recorder to "confirm" a story for the magazine.

It may be argued that *Confidential* dealt with celebrities, who are always in the public eye and therefore less entitled to privacy than others. And it is true that the courts feel their style of life to be an implicit consent to some publicity. But publicity is one thing; restrained gossip is another; and the concentration on prurient details that brought the magazine over 4,000,000 readers in its peak years is something else again. A few victims did sue, but most of them who might have launched libel, slander or invasion of privacy suits were intimidated by the danger that a court fight would bring on more exposure and sensationalism.

As soon as *Confidential* itself was dragged through the mud in several criminal trials the readership quickly began to dwindle; splattering dirt has a way of finally dirtying everyone who comes within range.

Though it has been six years now since the demise of the old *Confidential,* there are still lessons to be gained from it. While it held sway the film colony lived in fear from issue to issue, and the one overriding question of the day was, "Who will be next?" (It must be admitted, however, that Hollywood also grabbed up each issue as it came out on the newsstands.) The success of the magazine inspired a factory employee to turn out a mimeographed scandal sheet detailing the carryings-on in his plant, until he was caught and fired. It encouraged the spawning of a spate of imitators, some of which are still holding forth in the old tradition, though without the electronic gadgetry, the flamboyancy, or the circulation of the original. The greatest harm done by *Confidential,* I think, is that the shockingly widespread acceptance and sanction it received from the public for so long worked unconsciously upon our society to alienate us still further from a valuation of privacy.

12. Your Name Is Somebody Else's Fortune

> *We've got you on a list,*
> *We've got you on a list,*
> *and you NEVER WILL BE MISSED!*
> *—slogan in the Dunhill mailing list catalog*

IN JANUARY 1962, a California couple contemplated the 100 or so pieces of unsolicited ads, circulars, promotional brochures and other direct mail appeals that flooded their mailbox every month and decided they wanted very much to be missed. Thus began a campaign unique enough to become the subject of a UPI dispatch that was picked up by *The New York Times,* New York *Herald Tribune* and other papers.

What the couple did was set up a large empty box on their front porch and mark it FOR DEPOSIT JUNK MAIL. Then they invited all their friends and acquaintances to fill the box with their own unwanted direct mail advertising. The response was unexpected. As word spread, not only friends but even total strangers began to make their little contributions of junk mail. In no time the box was stuffed. Garbage cans, cartons and clothes baskets were added—and quickly piled high with the unwanted third-class mail.

Concluding their citizens' protest campaign, the couple packaged the donations and shipped them off to the Postmaster General of the United States. "I know the big mailing services have a powerful Washington lobby, but I think this is worth trying," they are quoted as saying. It was their hope that other communities—also fed up with the nuisance of such mail and its cost to the taxpayers—would institute similar campaigns.

Since the nation has not responded *en masse* (though, as we shall see, there have been other protests), it must be concluded that their hope still remains unfulfilled.

This lack of concerted effort is far from surprising. The intrusion into our mailboxes is, as anthropologist Ashley Montagu has pointed out, "after all one of the minor invasions" of privacy. More relevant to our understanding of the Goldfish Age is a question many of the contributors must have asked themselves as they dropped their junk mail into the California couple's garbage can. Indeed, it is a question practically every recipient of unrequested advertising matter asks: "How did I get on so many mail order lists?"

The answer lies in the methods and techniques of the industry that makes its $400-million-a-year living peddling your name to any and all comers. It is an incredible industry, at once utterly brazen and fascinatingly ingenious. It sifts through your likes and dislikes, examines the nature of your purchases, and scrutinizes your religious and social affiliations. It looks into the kind of work you do, analyzes your sports and hobbies, delves into the type of magazines you buy, even shows keen interest if you are engaged, married or about to enter the state of parenthood. Then, having completely denuded you, the industry places your name alongside thousands of others of similar background, like so many butterflies pinned to a tray. It is the industry of the list makers— the compilers, renters and sellers of names.

There is no better way of spotlighting the list makers' interest in you than by browsing through one of their catalogs. The one I have at hand at the moment is a 100-page booklet attractively put out by the Dunhill International List Co., Inc. This firm is one of the biggest compilers in the business. The catalog contains some 5,000 lists, just a portion of the 12,500 lists and 40 million names the Dunhill people have available.

Are you a high school graduating senior from Illinois? One of the 1,000,000 Jewish businessmen? A woman who has purchased apothecary jars? A railroad industry executive? One of 7,000,000 homeowners? You will likely be on at least one list.

The diversity is astounding. You may find yourself in company with 95,000 other buyers of wallet photos. Or among 9,150 presidents and program chairmen of women's clubs. Or with 549,140 persons who contributed to wildlife conservations.

Nothing is held sacred. Perhaps you are one of 48,000 "men and women of large means." Or among 110,000 women who "sent for booklet on child's trainer seat." Or among the 84,000 "older men who bought gadget to enhance sex life." Or one of the 23,000 "women who bought bust developer." Whatever your special interest, the compilers will find out, list you, offer you for sale. Today two out of every three persons are on at least one list, most on several. Today one out of every three letters in the average family's daily mail is an advertisement, sent at the third-class postal rate of a fraction over 2½¢ per piece.

The dispatch and efficiency of the list makers is amazing. Compilers are, in a sense, instant investigators. They have to be. Many lists are as perishable as yesterday's catch of fish. There is a story that a young wife learned she was pregnant and rushed home to tell her husband—only to find a diaper service salesman already there, trying to sign him up. A list maker had provided the salesman with the expectant mother's name. The story is probably apocryphal, but not by much.

Though they really are investigators in that they utilize some of the methods of private detectives, list makers do not consider themselves as such. When I told one highly experienced compiler that he was a pretty shrewd detective, he seemed surprised. He also seemed pleased. He had just finished telling me that he had informants in several of New York's biggest hospitals, as well as a man in the New York Health Department. These informants make a few dollars selling him names of people going into surgery, expectant mothers, new births. *Newsweek* quotes a Los Angeles compiler as saying,

"Some we buy under the table. You just got to know the right places to go."

One of the best places to go is the county clerk's office almost anywhere in the U.S. Normally, little or nothing handled by the county clerk is confidential information. As we have already seen, marriage licenses and business licenses are open to inspection. So is information on voters, mortgages, probated wills, etc. Of course, it is one thing for a record to be public, and quite another for the information to be compiled by county clerks for sale to the list makers. But the county clerks—or their subordinates—who make a personal profit refuse to see the distinction. According to Mr. Herbert Odza, former president of Dunhill, county clerks almost universally follow the practice of selling names and addresses. "The county clerkship," he added, "is the most profitable plum any political machine can offer."

Mr. Odza spoke from a lifetime's experience in the direct mail field. His relationship with county clerks has always been a happy one. For instance, county clerks have helped him compile highly profitable lists of stockholders in more than 1,000 gilt-edged American corporations. Stockholder lists are not that easy to come by. Neither corporations nor the Security & Exchange Commission will release shareholders' names. How do the county clerks get into the picture? By legally rounding up all of the proxies after a stockholders' battle is over, then—again legally—making these available as part of the public record.

Compilers are nothing if not ingenious in the way they come up with supposedly personal information. *Columbia,* the Knights of Columbus Magazine, has told of the way Odza provides name-and-address lists of wealthy families anywhere. Even—if it is requested—on a block-by-block basis. He began by getting nonprofit trade groups such as the Fifth Avenue Association to write to local Chambers of Commerce for him. The Chambers of Commerce submitted city maps. On these maps the areas in which the financially substantial citizens live were blocked out. Often the obliging C of C has even indicated the specific income bracket. The only thing missing were the addresses. Odza got those by contacting print shops in the particular area desired. The print shops used city directories in providing addresses.

During my interview with Odza he let the door slip ajar on a few more compiling secrets. Some direct mail advertisers prefer to narrow their market to include only persons living in older houses. The advertisers who voice this preference are usually selling some relatively expensive item that will likely be bought on time. Their theory is that residents of older apartment houses are much better credit risks than individuals who live in expensive new apartment buildings, buy everything on credit, and move frequently. How does a compiler segregate people by the age of the building they live in? By going to the city building department and looking through the census tracts. These show when each structure was built.

Odza's ingenuity displayed itself grandly the time a travel agency client wanted a list of passengers who had flown in jets. Airlines do not release names of passengers, either current or past. Odza approached several European airlines that flew across the equator and talked them into a gimmick. On each flight crossing the equator, the airlines distributed cards offering free certificates commemorating the equatorial crossing. All the passenger had to do was write in for the card. The stunt worked. Thousands of passengers wrote in. Odza provided the cards, the certificates—and compiled his list of jet passengers.

A European firm wanted a list of several thousand of America's best-dressed women. How would you pick them? This was Odza's way: he got a clipping service to provide newspaper accounts of touring opera premieres in various cities. Prominent men and women attending were usually listed. On the theory that these were also the best-dressed in town, he used them to compile his list.

Newspapers are generally a valuable source of information. Like the investigators, list makers either have their own staff clip out items of interest or, more often, subscribe to clipping bureaus. Many graduation, engagement and wedding lists are compiled via newspaper clips.

The old refrain we have already encountered so often before—the one that goes, "Everybody talks"—runs through the list maker's business, too. Are you a newlywed who recently used the services of a travel bureau or resort hotel? Be advised that likely someone in either establishment has sold your name to a mailing list house. It, in turn, will sell it to insurance companies, furniture dealers, savings banks, or any other direct mail advertiser who thinks he can do business with you. If you have just moved into a new community, chances are good the moving company has tipped off a mailing list house to the fact that you are a new arrival. If you have recently become a subscriber of the Bell Telephone Company of Pennsylvania, take it for granted that your name is already on somebody's list: this Bell unit sells daily lists of its new subscribers. (It is the only Bell company that does.)

Pharmacists also do a lot of talking. William Michelfelder tells in his book *It's Cheaper to Die* how Fisher-Stevens, Inc., and other direct mail companies sell lists of physicians' names most seen on pharmaceutical blanks to pharmaceutical manufacturers. The information is passed on to the detail men who make the rounds of physicians' offices. Thus, the detail man who tries to persuade a physician to order more of his products knows whether he is talking to a "high-volume prescriber."

Traffic is brisk in lists of college students. Schools do not, as a rule, release their roster of enrollments. However, this fact does not discourage the list makers. They write to each school for the name of the leader of the junior class, indicating that they wish to offer him employment. Once a list maker has the class leader's name, he contacts the boy directly, offering to pay him for compiling the names and addresses of the boys and girls in his class. It almost always works.

Names of graduating seniors are easier to get, for they are listed in school yearbooks. In fact, yearbooks, alumni association rosters, social and fraternal organization rosters, social registers, Who's Who directories, city directories, membership lists of professional societies and dozens of other directories of all kinds are the most obvious sources for the compilers. O. E. McIntyre Inc. of New York is a master dissector of telephone books. R. L. Polk & Co. of Detroit compiles car registration lists from all over the U.S., breaking them down geographically and every other way, another example of public records being used for strictly commercial purposes.

Compilation of religious lists is a different kettle of names. They are not available through public documents, nor do churches and synagogues release the names of parishioners. Nevertheless, there is a flourishing business in the sale of religious lists both for fund raising and other purposes. For instance, the Catholic Laity Bureau of New Jersey advertises half a million Catholic men and women. Names are broken down into ten categories, such as executives, wealthy widows and single women. Two sources for Catholic names are religious shops and Catholic societies.

One large mailing list house serves hotels and a few large business firms that will not cater to or hire Negroes, Jews or Catholics. The list house cannot guarantee completely uncontaminated lists but does its best to purge them of undesirables by screening the names beforehand. All obviously Jewish-sounding names are eliminated. So are persons from predominantly Jewish, Negro, Irish or Italian neighborhoods.

On the other hand, as the Negro purchasing power grows stronger, list houses may find a popular demand for lists containing *only* Negroes. The February 1963 issue of *The Reporter of Direct Mail Advertising* devoted five pages to the Negro market. Though Negroes account for some 10 percent of all consumer goods sold in the U.S., no more than 2 percent of the nation's advertising budget is spent on ads aimed directly at the Negro. To date, mailing list houses report little demand for exclusively Negro lists. But a few companies have begun testing Negro response to mail order solicitation, among them the Columbia Record Club.

Executives, the most aggressively investigated group of all, are a prime mail order target. Lists of executives, either composite or pinpointed by industry, are sold as often as 40 times a year by the same mail order company.

Millionaire lists are, by contrast, distinctly unpopular. Few millionaires are given to mail order buying; fewer still receive their mail until it is screened by secretaries. Nevertheless, one famous New York jeweler periodically buys millionaire lists that include items such as millionaires' wives' birthday dates. He then writes the millionaire a personal letter reminding him that his wife's birthday is coming up soon, and wouldn't a nice $50,000 bracelet make a lovely birthday gift? The jeweler makes a lot of important sales this way. In general, however, lists of American millionaires are more popular in England, where they are being sold for $25 to husband-seeking girls of a decidedly optimistic cast.

Americans of all economic ranks will find their mailboxes increasingly invaded by foreign advertising matter as well as the domestic variety. Ten years ago Dunhill had practically no foreign clients. Now it does nearly 15 percent of its business with overseas firms. The *Wall Street Journal* reports that Dunhill recently sold the names of 2,000,000 Americans to Air France; also 200,000 names of executives living in small towns, to a Hong Kong tailor.

There is another important factor that contributes to the glut of advertising matter in your mailbox. Lists of names are not only compiled, but already-existing lists are rented and swapped. A magazine may rent its subscription list to book publishers, record clubs or a dozen other non-competing mail order enterprises. A business school may rent the names of every person who answered its ad.

The owner of an especially valuable list of regular mail order purchasers may earn himself a substantial rental income. It is far from unusual for that income to run into six figures annually. Owners and renters of lists are brought together through the good offices of the mailing list brokers, of whom there are some 200 in the U.S. According to a brochure of the National Council of Mailing List Brokers, "Throughout the country brokers are constantly checking with all conceivable sources to locate organizations which can benefit by allowing their lists to be used on a one-time rental basis by reputable, specialized (and usually noncompetitive) mailers."

Newsweek tells of New York's Lewis Kleid Co., one of the largest brokers in the U.S. Kleid handles some 125 million names a year, his lists ranging in size from the Phi Beta Kappa Association to the million-member Diner's Club. The names rent for about $20 per 1,000, of which Kleid gets 20 percent. The Diner's Club earns about $200,000 a year by renting its mailing list.

The Diner's Club is not alone in releasing its membership list to other firms. The Direct Mail Advertising Association indicates that all of the credit card companies indulge in this practice. Treating what might be assumed to be confidential lists of credit customers as salable products has turned into a lucrative business.

When a concern rents out its mailing list it usually does so on a one-shot basis, arranging to have its broker handle the actual addressing of envelopes for the renter. The renter never sees the actual list, thus minimizing for the concern the risk of having its names used again without payment. However, the renter's inability to cull or clean the list in any way brings on problems. He may—and frequently does—duplicate his mailings. In a nation continually on the move, "nixies"—undeliverable items—are a great big headache for all segments of the industry. The post office will advise a mailer of any change of address or other reason for nondelivery, but at 8¢ per piece it's an expensive proposition. Comparatively few third-class envelopes carry the notation, RETURN REQUESTED.

Another headache is the accidental mismatching of advertiser with recipient. For instance, one man complained to *The Reporter of Direct Mail Advertising* about the fact that his twelve-year-old son was receiving circulars urging him

142

to subscribe to a magazine about Florida real estate. The letter writer happened to be a former president of the Direct Mail Advertising Association and decried the poor public relations value of such incidents which, he said, occur too often.

The direct mail industry is quite sensitive to its public image. The words "junk mail" are anathema and officially referred to only by their initials. Apparently unwilling to believe that a flood of high-pressure direct mail in the nation's mailboxes can be injurious to its public relations, the industry seems prone to lump all its critics in the screwball category. Its theme is, "People love to get mail of any kind." Thus a spokesman for the Direct Mail Advertising Association, insisting there could be no saturation point either for addressed third-class mail or "buckshot" (occupant) mailings, told me that one of the Association's important functions is to "combat cranks, objectors, and bad personal publicity."

Perhaps even more pointed is this suggestion offered to the readers of *The Reporter of Direct Mail Advertising* by one disciple: "To reach the crackpots who resent j____ m____ provide a space for checking, 'I do not want to receive your promotional mail. Please take my name off the list.'"

However, in the summer of 1962 "crackpots" suddenly seemed to abound. Some, in an effort to stem an especially heavy tide of third-class mail during that period, wrote REFUSED on envelopes marked RETURN REQUESTED. This cost the senders money for each piece of mail returned. Other objectors sent back business-reply envelopes with angry notes or nothing but air inside. A few even returned the envelopes with weights of one kind or another inside—a stunt that, incidentally, is contrary to post office regulations.

The "crackpots" have been numerous enough to encourage Congressman Morris K. Udall (D., Ariz.) to sponsor a bill that would afford postal patrons greater control over what is dropped in their mailbox. Introduced (for the second time) in January 1963, the bill would give every person the right to return to the post office any piece of unsolicited mail received, together with a request that his name and address be removed from the mailing list. Sanctions would be imposed on any sender ignoring the request.

The bill, if passed, would obviously be chaotic to the direct mail industry—what with the endless passing back and forth of lists. The industry would have to revamp its present system extensively. An alternative is a higher postal rate for third-class mail. But not to worry. As that California couple pointed out, the industry has a powerful Washington lobby; it can take care of itself.

Nevertheless, it is refreshing to hear a legislator speak aloud on the individual's right to privacy. Two legislators, in fact. A similar bill was introduced in 1962 by Representatives Udall and Glenn Cunningham of Nebraska.

At that time the Congressmen said, "The American postal patron has for too long a time been the captive of the mass mailer. 'A man's home is his castle' and he should be guaranteed the right to protect his home and his family from outside invasion from whatever source." Arguing that each person should have the means not only to refuse mail but to assure that he will not continue to be deluged by it, the Congressmen added, "We firmly believe that a person's mailbox should be as inviolate as his home and that he should have the same right of determination with regard to it as he now has with all other forms of communication."

In the Goldfish Age, such publicly uttered sentiments sound positively heretical.

13. Fund-Raising and Your Privacy

AMERICANS HAVE ALWAYS been highly responsive givers. No other nation in the world has a greater tradition of philanthropy, no other people have a greater reputation for donating to worthy causes. Even foreign critics ready to see the worst in all Americans often concede that we are—collectively and individually—"generous."

Indeed, this sense of generosity is one of our great and wonderful strengths of national character. And it has been a continuingly creative and constructive force in terms of the welfare of our communities. In fact, many of our most valuable institutions have grown out of philanthropy.

Yet within the past couple of decades a paradox has come to life. On the one hand, charitable contributions have climbed to an all-time high. Figures compiled by the American Association of Fund-Raising Counsel, Inc. (AAFRC) show that in 1962 the American people contributed $9.2 billion to philanthropy.* So vast is this sum, it places philanthropy—at least in dollar value—among our top five industries.

Philanthropy is not really an industry, of course, and it would be a sad thing if we were all finally to look at it as such. Yet philanthropy, altruism, charity—however you want to call it, this impulse to do something for the other person (or, collectively, for all of us) is taking place in an increasingly uncharitable atmosphere. Giving used to be somewhat spontaneous; very largely a private affair; and wholly, intensely personal. No more. Giving has not escaped the ethics of the community; on the contrary, it has become almost totally subject to the ground rules and dismaying tensions of the Goldfish Age.

Since contributions adding up to nearly ten billion dollars can hardly be raised by amateurs, the ground rules are made up by the experts—the shrewd, intelligent, highly trained professional fund raisers of whom *Business Week* has said, in what is surely understatement, "You'll find that many have a surprising grasp of sound business principles." Their philosophy is perhaps best expressed by an anonymous fund raiser quoted in Richard Carter's *The Gentle Legions* (a book written in praise of the voluntary national health organizations). This expert said, "People need to be pressured. They don't automatically give to good causes. If they gave automatically, I could rent a store, put a sign in the window, lock the door, and let them throw the money over the transom."

No, money is not thrown over the transom. It is extracted from the donor in campaigns as intricate and carefully conceived as any coming out of Madison Avenue—campaigns that utilize the latest, most effective techniques of psychology, high-pressure promotion and manipulation. This pragmatic approach to "sweet charity" holds true for all three categories of fund-raising: 1) the professional fund-raising firms that have been a powerful influence in persuading wealthier donors to contribute money for schools, hospitals, churches and other social institutions; 2) the voluntary national health organizations that solicit mainly on a door-to-door basis; 3) the United Fund and Community Chest campaigns that make their pitch in the work place, collecting mainly through payroll deduction plans. We will consider all three, from the standpoint of privacy.

The professional fund-raising firms give us a good indica-

* AAFRC figures show that religious giving accounted for just about half that $9.2 billion.

tion of just how big and complex American philanthropy has become. Their function is to analyze and manage the fund-raising efforts of nonprofit institutions. According to Mr. Eldredge Hiller, executive director of the AAFRC, there are about 400 of these professional firms scattered throughout the U.S. However, only about 75 meet AAFRC standards, and only 28 fund-raising firms are actually members. Among the various points listed in the AAFRC Fair Practices Code are admonitions against using "methods harmful to the public" and giving kickbacks.

Professional fund raisers usually try to remain in the background while conducting a campaign. This is less an expression of innate modesty than a recognition of the fact that donors and volunteers are much more responsive if an "outsider" is not obviously involved in the campaign proceedings. Many a successful campaign has come and gone with only a handful of people—the administrative committee—aware that a staff of experts directed the whole show.

The show itself is—as to an extent it must be—an extravaganza of intrusive techniques. Let's say you and a group of your friends have decided to establish a Foundation for Good Works (henceforth to be known as Foundation). You approach a professional fund-raising counselor. His first step is to conduct a preliminary investigation. He will want to satisfy himself on the following points: Does your case have public appeal, are there enough people interested in the idea of the Foundation? Can you get leaders for the campaign, persons with influence and prestige in the community? Are there enough wealthy persons around who can be counted on as potential donors? (The general public would be approached, of course; but wealthy contributors are the "pacesetters" and usually donate at least 60 percent of the desired goal.) Are there sufficient numbers of volunteers available to do the actual collecting? Finally, does your group have enough "seed money"—the funds necessary to underwrite the entire campaign costs, including the fund raiser's fee?*

If the answer to all of these questions is a resounding yes, the pro goes ahead with the blueprinting of the campaign. Most important of all is the naming of the front man—the chairman of the campaign, always someone whose name com-

---

* The AAFRC specifies that "member firms do business only on the basis of a specified fee, determined prior to the beginning of the campaign. They will not serve clients on the unprofessional basis of a percentage or commission of the sums raised."

mands respect and attention in the community. A man who was picked to head a drive to establish a hospital in pre-Communist China told me the fund raiser groomed him "as carefully as though I were being elevated to stardom." One of the ploys used was the getting out of an impressive brochure; it listed the objectives of the campaign, showed pictures and sketches of children and elderly people in the proposed hospital, contained a number of statements attributed to the chairman.

"I had really made none of those statements," he recalls, "the whole thing was a surprise to me." But he admitted that the remarks he was supposed to have made were quite good. In fact, they impressed him so much he okayed their use. A surprisingly small amount of the text dealt with the actual hospital. Much space was devoted to keeping China from going Red; raising the level of health of the Chinese population; extending the influence of the church group sponsoring this campaign. By the time the text got down to the hospital itself, the project would, in the eyes of the prospective donor reading through the brochure, have assumed much larger dimensions than merely the building of one hospital in a remote city belonging to a far-off land.

This is in line with accepted professional fund-raising practice. A veteran fund raiser, David M. Church, has written that "interest is created by the compelling generality and then directed toward a specific idea." Among other tips offered by Mr. Church is the suggestion that ideas need to be repeated, for slogans "penetrate the public mind."

Once the chairman, treasurer and other officials of your Foundation campaign are selected, the fund raiser's next step is to organize the various committees for publicity, corporate gifts, special gifts, lists & quotas, etc.

The lists and quotas committee is the investigative arm of the campaign, and those of you on it get together to discuss all of the possible donors, particularly the ones who can be counted on to make substantial contributions. But that is only the beginning.

Next to each name you would put down every bit of personal information you could associate with the person: his age, marital status, children, likes and dislikes, hobbies, prejudices, financial interests, social or political affiliations, and how he has responded to other fund-raising appeals. You would jot down his vulnerabilities and what would seem to be the most effective way of getting through to his wallet. You would note the names of people close to him, or of people who know people close to him, so that perhaps one of them could be used for the actual soliciting. The contact has always to be on the same or higher social level, for a cardinal fund-raising rule has it that a high-level giver is never approached by someone on a lower echelon. Finally, in making up the file card on your prospect, you would jot down just how much of a bite he would be good for.

All this sounds like a lot of trouble, not to mention intrusion. But it brings results. Writer John Wieting noted in *The American Mercury* that as much care may go into developing one wealthy prospect as in a drive covering an entire town. One fund-raising firm spent $700 presenting a case to a single man. It was a worthwhile investment, netting the campaign a check for $550,000.

The fund raiser who agrees to mastermind a campaign does not come empty-handed. He has his own extensive dossiers, both of individuals and organizations. His files contain reams of information on foundations, trust funds, estates, business and industrial firms. Most professionals maintain actual research staffs that may number half-a-dozen or more people. The staff scans newspapers and magazines from all over the country. Has Mr. A made a statement that a liberal arts college is needed for engineers? A file is made up on Mr. A, if none already exists. Then, if a liberal arts college has a fund-raising drive, Mr. A would be a likely prospect. Is there an account of Mr. B's substantial contributions to an orphanage? Into the file he goes. Has Mr. C expressed concern for the state of some oppressed group? He too is clipped and a home made for him in the files. Announcements of society weddings, sales of mansions or yachts—everything is grist for the fund-raising mill.

In 1963 the long-established fund-raising firm of Marts & Lundy conducted a campaign for a New York hospital. Arnaud C. Marts, co-founder of the firm and one of the field's old-timers, described to me some of the ways his organization developed lists of donors. The firm looked for people who benefited from the hospital and people interested in the creation of a new health center. The hospital itself, as well as physicians practicing there, revealed the names of patients. Marts & Lundy's own files of foundations and corporations revealed which, in Mr. Marts's words, "will give to this cause, and which will hide."

Many professional fund raisers retain the files of individual donors developed in each specific campaign. This data is a big selling point when a new client comes along. The pro says, "You hire us and we can bring you a list of very generous persons who have given to other organizations." Thus, the donor's privacy is not only devalued at the time of the original appeal, it is also given short shrift subsequently. By the way, not all fund raisers consider it ethical to bandy about a contributor's name from campaign to campaign. Instead, they leave with the client the files accumulated during the campaign.

Dossiers as such, however, are an integral part of all fund-raising firms and ventures. Thus, inveterate fund raiser Eddie Cantor, revealing how he handles a money-raising cocktail party and dinner, explained, "Here I meet fifty or sixty top donors, and by the time they get there I know their fiscal history, the saps and branches of their family trees, their hobbies and their first names as well as I know my own."

The professional who has your Foundation campaign well along—and every other fund raiser—is a keen psychologist. He knows not only why a particular donor will give to a specific cause, but why people generally make charitable contributions. This information he uses in planning his strategy. Researchers outside the field have also conducted a number of important studies dealing with the question of why people give. The results provide both publicity and public relations experts with the necessary inspiration to write copy that will more effectively reach the donor's viscera.

The *Public Relations Journal* has carried an article by Dr. Sidney J. Levy of Social Research, Inc., on the impact made by various appeals. Levy's research showed that people are more likely to contribute to causes that make an emotional impact. But they will also give to other causes if they feel a sense of obligation to do so "much as they are obliged to pay taxes."

Levy found that the donor's loyalties begin with the church; go on to fraternal organizations, schools and other groups with which he has an association; are followed by "emotionally related organizations such as health groups, orphanages and old people's homes with which the donor can identify present or prospective interests"; winding up with such obligatory commitments as the Red Cross or Community Chest.

Levy noted that once a pattern of giving is established, the donor is likely to go on following it year after year, without varying the amount of the contribution. He saw some danger in this and advised public relations men, "In an economic ession period, they [the donors] will be ashamed to reduce their donations and therefore may drop the charity entirely. At such times, public relations men must take care that their appeals do not arouse anxieties that would trigger off this reaction." He added that the tendency to give the same amount each year must also be taken into account in attempts to increase donations.

The 1962 edition of *Giving USA,* a yearbook published by the American Association of Fund-Raising Counsel, contains a fascinating two-page lesson in philanthropic motivation and cultivation. There are three broad categories of givers listed: 1) those who are prompted by love of God, fellow man, or a sense of social responsibility; 2) repeaters—the habitual givers; 3) people whose giving is motivated by self-interest. Of course, there is probably a considerable amount of overlapping in most people, and appeals usually offer something to all three types.

The yearbook's outline is especially interesting in terms of how a donor's drives and anxieties can be used to motivate him into giving. The category of "self-interest," for example, is broken down into five parts. They are:

Fear. The fearful react to appeals that emphasize the dire results of *not* giving. Copy that hammers away at the theme of "three out of four will die," or "protect your home from . . ." is the most effective.

Self-protection. These are the superstitious, who consider it bad luck to refuse a fund-raising request. Copy might be slanted on the "Don't let this happen to your child" theme, and requests for money are most effective when the appeal is made by a social superior.

Self-aggrandizement. This category would include the socially ambitious "keeping up with the Joneses" type. Such donors are mainly stimulated by the promise of publicity. The juices of generosity also flow more freely when the contributors' lists (presumably with amounts donated) are made public.

Submission to pressure. Donors falling into this category act out of "fear of social and business criticism." They include the nouveau riche who always get the best table at a benefit ball. The yearbook notes that these people respond to "memorials, honor rolls, acknowledgments."

Tax advantage. Here we find the business go-getter who is acutely conscious of customer relations. No need for subtlety with him. A simple statement of tax advantages will stimulate the gift.

Dr. Levy's motivational study found that corporations are equally susceptible to the relationship between their contributions to philanthropy and their high-bracket income tax status. In addition, corporate self-interest includes an acceptance of civic responsibility. Discussing Community Funds, Levy states that campaign literature should explain how "money will be distributed among welfare agencies, what the new college physics building will mean to industrial research and development, what heart disease and alcoholism mean to business in terms of lost man-hours, early retirements and death benefits."

Following your Foundation's campaign through its progressions, we find that it is one of the few to gain acceptance in the business community. Out of a consideration for tax benefits, civic responsibility or a plain desire to present a good image, corporations in your area eagerly agree to conduct their own Foundation campaigns on your behalf. It might be well for you, then, to announce that a gold plaque will be awarded to the organization that comes up with the highest total of donations in relation to its size. This has proved to be quite an effective technique, as it serves to arouse the competitive spirit among the participating firms. Unfortunately, it also arouses somewhat less attractive feelings. An official of one of the watchdog agencies set up to police charitable organizations has seen these pressures in operation. He told me:

"There's an especially vicious situation where buyer-seller relationships exist in business. The buyer whose firm is participating in a fund-raising drive writes a letter to his principal suppliers requesting a contribution. This filters down to the level where the local liquor store is forced—by regular customers who are staging a fund-raising rally—to contribute cases of whisky."

A businessman related a situation in which similarly unsubtle forces played a role in eliciting his contribution. He was in the process of negotiating a business loan with his bank, which was at the time involved in a charity drive. The banker processing the loan dropped by one day and "invited" him to make a donation. He did. "But," he says, "afterwards I was sore about it. Sore with myself for submitting to that kind of extortion, I guess. The charity itself was worthwhile, no question about that. But the way I had to make my contribution left a sour taste."

Pressure can become just as intense within an organization, particularly if the boss is intent on getting that gold plaque. Suppose a particular department within the corporation has not come up to par in making its donations. What happens then, frequently, is that the top brass leans on the foreman. And the foreman in turn pressures his men to come up with the funds.

He has a number of ways of doing this. He might slap them on the back, the buddy-buddy approach. He might subtly imply that the would-be giver will stand in better favor with him if he contributes. He might hint that the reluctant employee would not only have his own conscience against him, but also his employer, his fellow workers, and his union. The foreman might, perhaps as a last resort, come around with a list of non-givers prepared by the payroll department. The fact that the list was actually prepared by the payroll people proves to be quite worrisome to some workers.

The foreman undoubtedly believes in the charity he is so zealously promoting. Yet it should be noted that quite likely his zeal is only partly motivated by altruism. He, no less than the other workers, wants to avoid getting in bad with the front office. Then, too, he wants to show the front office his capabilities as a leader, his ability to influence others. The job he does in the campaign may serve to secure or elevate his own status.

Fund-raising drives produce similar derivative rewards for the junior executive whose eyes are cast toward the corporate stars. He is indeed a fortunate young man whose company loans him out to work on a charity campaign. This is true even though his task may be grueling and have its distasteful aspects. One junior executive confessed after the conclusion of a local health drive in which he was one of the prime movers, "I think I expended more energy in those two months than I had the entire year previously." But, as he was the first to admit, all that effort paid off. It gave him a chance to demonstrate that he could operate successfully in a situation that involved stress, demanded leadership, required organizational abilities. In other words, it gave him a chance to display his talents without stepping on his superiors' toes.

As *Business Week* has pointed out, fund-raising drives give junior executives other advantages as well, namely the "chance to develop contacts and skills that usually take him years to build up in his regular job." The business magazine tells of one junior executive who returned from his fund-raising stint with a method to control absenteeism, a new safety measure, and a plant welfare plan. Your campaign, you see, sets all kinds of unexpected forces into motion.

At this point it might be well to leave your Foundation campaign (which I trust is flourishing) and explore what has come to be the most controversial, hostility-provoking, and intrusive aspect of the whole fund-raising field—the activities of the national health agencies and their bitter foe, the United Funds. We will also take a look at a few independent national charities and their methods.

In contrast to the professional fund raisers' focus on wealthier contributors, the national philanthropic agencies outside the United Fund framework go after everybody in direct mail or doorbell-ringing campaigns. While this difference in methodology might give the impression that the latter groups are less structured and tactical, hence more imbued with the homey touch, it is another instance of appearance being deceptive. Organization is just as tight, pressures to give just as strong.

Let's start with the Los Angeles branch of a very famous health agency that relies primarily on direct mail. The branch has an automatic data-processing machine large enough to rival those of medium-sized businesses. Every named contributor is tagged with an IBM card. The contributor is automatically contacted the following year. Whether he gives is noted from year to year.

The person who gives though he has moved elsewhere is put on a special star list. This means that he is characterized as a self-starter and bombarded with special letters. With its advanced business machines, the health agency is able to survey the Los Angeles area neighborhood by neighborhood. If a particular housing development is a "low giver," it comes in for special attention. Which usually means door-to-door canvassing.

The December 1961 issue of *Business Automation* tells of a charity that is an even greater marvel of efficiency. This is the Salvatorian Center, the fund-raising arm of the Society of the Divine Saviour, a Catholic order dating back to 1881. The Center raises money for 7 American seminaries, numerous foreign missions, three Southern Negro and five American-Indian missions. Collections for these far-flung charitable enterprises are made via the direct mail method.

Business Automation explains that the Salvatorian mailing list, far more than a mere directory of names and addresses, is actually a "carefully controlled collection of 'personal histories' on every one of their past benefactors. Recorded and maintained on magnetic tape, each of these histories contains 341 characters of coded information on the donor,

153

including when he was last solicited, how long it took him to respond, the type of appeal to which he responded, the size of his contribution, his total donations during the year, and similar data."

The Center does not use outside compilers. It keeps adding to its list from within, for current benefactors submit names of potential donors. Appeals are made for money or for the promotion of some item such as cheese, Christmas cards or religious artifacts, but donors are not bombarded for every campaign. Explained Father Alfred Schmidt, executive director of the Salvatorian Center, "By electronically sorting through our files, we can pick out a choice mailing list comprising names of donors whose past histories indicate that they will be receptive to the type of appeal we have in mind."

The Center is geared to handle a daily output of up to 100,000 names. It follows up on each donation. Every benefactor receives a "personal" letter of thanks from Father Alfred. Such letters are written on 7 batteries of automatic typewriters, every letter signed by an automatic pen. Unanswered appeals are also handled as efficiently. The would-be donors are sent reminder letters every 30 days.

The Salvatorian Center's mailing list, the key to its projects, is carefully guarded. It refuses to rent or sell its list to any other organization. That in itself makes it unusual. At one time every fund-raising group kept its mailing list under lock and key, but times have changed. They have changed because the charity organizations have discovered the phenomenon of "conditioned giving." A charity official gave me his private interpretation of that term: "It's like the cow that gives milk as long as it's stimulated. The feeling now is that it's better for everybody concerned if they can keep people on the giving kick." When a health agency or charitable group rents out its mailing list, it does so only at those times of the year that do not conflict with its own drive, however.

Mailing lists are not only rented or traded with other philanthropic organizations, they are also sold to the mailing list compilers. When I questioned a compiler about that, he said, "Most of the fund-raising groups sell lists of donors to us. They're very aggressive about it. Selling those names is a big industry with them."

Thus it may please you to know that when you send a donation check through the mail you are actually contributing twice—first your money, then your name. The same thing may well happen if you contribute to a campaign masterminded by a professional fund raiser. Arnaud Marts, who disapproves strongly of the practice, admits that a number of professional fund raisers sell names of contributors to institutions that cannot or will not hire the professional himself. Some readers may conclude—along with some observers in the philanthropy field—that when a list of contributors is released for *any* reason it is engaging both in an invasion of privacy and a betrayal of trust.

An even more questionable practice is mailing out unsolicited merchandise. Some charitable organizations send greeting cards, neckties, key chains, license plate replicas, identification tags, and even the Lord's Prayer on a pinhead through the mails to prospective donors in hope of evoking a charitable response. Many of the Better Business Bureaus, the National Information Bureau (a nonprofit agency that investigates and sets standards for philanthropic organizations), and the Direct Mail Advertising Association frown on the practice. The objections are at least partly based on practical considerations. These were pointed up by Mr. A. B. Johnston, executive vice-president of the Chicago Better Business Bureau, in a letter to *The Reporter of Direct Mail Advertising*. According to Mr. Johnston, "Few, if any, donors recognize that only a pitifully small portion of the dollar they forward in response to charity or welfare appeals involving unordered merchandise, actually reaches the charity for which the solicitation is made." The Chicago Better Business Bureau official went on to state that when the soliciting agents are asked to provide a breakdown of their costs, they are seldom frank in revealing how much of the moneys collected actually reach the charity for which it was intended. Even if a breakdown is provided, he noted, "it is often so confusing it is of no value."

A case point is Amvets, which sent $1.25 neckties to prospective donors, as unordered merchandise. The charity reportedly allowed a commercial enterprise to handle the neckties under contract, and received only a fraction of the money that came in. *The Reporter of Direct Mail Advertising*, which gave an account of the Amvets' necktie tale, said the charity sent dunning letters to people who did not respond. Post office regulations are not sympathetic to such maneuvers. They provide that the recipient of unsolicited merchandise is neither obligated to return the item nor pay for it, if he does not use it.

D. Paul Reed, executive director of the National Information Bureau, points up the moral issue involved in the sending of unsolicited merchandise. Charities that engage in the practice, he feels, base their operation on the "high standard of responsibility characteristic of most Americans, who feel obligated to pay for this merchandise they neither wanted nor ordered."

Another critic of the manipulative approach to fund-raising was prepared to go even further. Our discussion involved all kinds of direct mail appeals, not only those hinging on unordered merchandise. This critic focused his sights on what might at first seem like a trifling technique: charities that enclose reply envelopes with real uncanceled stamps already pasted on, rather than the more often used business reply envelopes. The technique is calculated, he feels: an added bit pressure. People feel more obligated to respond when they see a 5¢ stamp pasted on the reply envelope. They get the feeling that "they have the organization's money in their own hand." Of course, not everybody responds nobly. Some frugal souls simply soak off the stamp and use it for their personal mail.

Many charitable organizations and most national health agencies skip direct mail for what they consider a more effective form of fund-raising: door-to-door solicitation. (A notable exception is the National Tuberculosis Association, whose Christmas seals have become as familiar a sight in December as the Salvation Army bell-ringers.) Door-to-door soliciting, which is done by volunteers, is generally (though not always) less expensive than direct mail. It also offers a more pointed form of pressure-to-give than circulars found in the mailbox: a direct mail appeal, even with a real-life stamp stuck on the reply envelope, is easier to disregard than the neighbor who stares you accusingly in the eye.

The coercive force of the neighbor who comes to collect is felt particularly in cities like New York; there, whenever possible, each apartment building has its own resident volunteer collector. The apartment dwellers usually give something, even if the cause being solicited does not really appeal to them. It is awfully difficult to say no to the man or woman whom you meet in the elevator each day, or pass in the hall as you go in and out of the building. And they do work hard, these volunteers, under sometimes difficult conditions, for a cause they truly believe in.

But some volunteer collectors for the health agencies enhance the pressure their presence naturally creates by being personally aggressive. A few months ago one of the neighbors in my New York apartment building solicited for a major charitable organization. The cause, while unquestionably worthy in its own right, was one to which I personally did not respond. I decided, for the first time, to ignore the little solicitation envelope the neighbor had slipped under the door. Ten days later he paid me a short visit and asked for a contribution. When I told him I preferred to skip this one, he glowered and demanded, "Were you afraid to tell me?"

Other people have told me of similar experiences. A get-tough attitude, a desire to collect money at all costs, merely creates resentment and underscores the pressure already implicit in this form of collecting.

Health agencies, by the way, do not depend entirely on the small giver. In point of fact, a substantial portion of each campaign's goal arrives in the form of special gifts made by wealthy contributors. Like the professional fund-raising firms —on whom they also call for help—the national health organizations have their own lists of prospects.

Richard Carter tells of these lists in his *The Gentle Legions*. They are composed of names of persons who have "made generous memorial bequests, have achieved wealth or prominence in the community, have joined an exclusive club, have retired in comfort, or have inherited a lot of money." The health agency going after a substantial would-be contributor first butters him up by sending him literature, inviting him to serve as a volunteer, and having other influential people of means discuss the agency's program with him. The solicitor who is to make the actual appeal is carefully chosen. Mr. Carter tells of a Cancer Society manual that lists the solicitors it has found most effective: "cured cancer patients, past contributors of large gifts, bank and industrial executives," among others.

The intrusive aspect of fund-raising that has received the most publicity—and condemnation—is the multiplicity of campaigns. For instance, the now-defunct *American Magazine* ran an article titled, "Are Charity Drives Driving You Crazy?" *Good Housekeeping* printed a piece called, "The Race for Your Charity Dollars." *The Wall Street Journal* quoted Dr. Robert H. Hamlin, of Harvard University's School of Public Health, as saying, "We might get so many solicitations eventually that it will kill the goose that laid the golden egg."

Few householders repeatedly bombarded with appeals would argue the point. In January, appeals come from the National Foundation (March of Dimes) and United Cerebral Palsy Assoc., in February they come from the American

Heart Association and the National Hemophilia Association; in March from the Leukemia Society, the American Red Cross, the National Society for Crippled Children & Adults; in April from the American Cancer Society and the Myasthenia Gravis Foundation; in May from the National Association of Mental Health and the National Multiple Sclerosis Society.

There is a summer hiatus, then the campaign begins anew in September, with the Arthritis & Rheumatism Foundation and the National Cystic Fibrosis Research Foundation. Thanksgiving through Labor Day sees the United Funds and Community Chests and the Muscular Dystrophy Association (in October). November brings the National Association for Retarded Children and the windup in December comes with the National Tuberculosis Association.*

Records of the National Information Bureau show that in 1963 there were 37 major national health agencies in existence. Close to 50 percent did not exist in 1945. The proliferation of the health agencies has created some of the most disturbing problems in the whole field of philanthropy. To their founders and most enthusiastic followers, a majority of whom have some personal relationship with the disease that occupies their interests, every one of these agencies fulfills an urgent public need. They sponsor research, provide medical care, educate the public and needle the Government into providing more medical research funds.

Nevertheless, the public at large, subjected to a seemingly endless barrage of high-pressure appeals, has been asking questions that are in themselves becoming more and more urgent. Is it really necessary to have, as one critic aptly put it, "practically an agency for each disease?" Isn't there a significant amount of overlapping in the work and the goals of all these agencies? Doesn't the scramble for the charity dollar increase the pressure on donor and volunteer, increase the cost of putting on a campaign, reduce the funds available for actual research and the care of the sick?

The multiplicity of campaigns—which include not only those conducted by the health agencies but by countless other worthy national and local institutions, as well—has provoked bitter competition for *time* as well as for money.

Volunteerism is very much a part of the American tradition, beginning with the pioneers' concept of neighbor help-

* Not all of these agencies collect separately in every community.

ing neighbor. A 1962 survey conducted by AAFRC shows that 35 national philanthropic agencies had over 32,000,000 listed volunteers. Include church workers and thousands of men and women who volunteer on strictly local campaigns, and you have a total of over 50,000,000 volunteers. A significant number of volunteers work on behalf of several agencies, of course, and the total includes many millions who are not involved in actual fund-raising. Even so, the number of people available for soliciting is vast. Yet the demand caused by the proliferating agencies exceeds the supply.

And the problem is growing worse. The National Information Bureau tells of the housewife who received requests from three separate philanthropic organizations in a single day, each requesting her help in soliciting contributions from her neighbors. As a result of the pressure, she refused to serve even on behalf of the organization for which she had solicited the year before. Admitting that fund-raisers are finding it more difficult to get volunteers, a Marts & Lundy official stated, a trifle ruefully, "Part of our job is to get people to do the things they don't want to." And Henry Webber, associate executive director of United Community Funds and Councils of America, said flatly, "People are being besieged by requests to become volunteers."

A friend who lives in a 36-unit apartment building in New York told me she was telephoned by a representative for one of the best-known national health agencies, asking her to act as the collector in her building. My friend declined, explaining that she was both working and taking care of a child. She reports that the party on the other end of the line grew a bit indignant and finally said, "You were my last hope—everybody else in the building has refused."

The remark might merely have been a softening-up device. Many philanthropic organizations are now having such a tough time getting volunteers, they have developed a new system. They hire former telephone operators as *paid* solicitors whose sole job it is to sit by the telephone and talk housewives into volunteering.

United Funds and Community Chests grew out of a grassroots expression for more order in philanthropy. With their plan of one solicitation a year on behalf of an amalgam of charities, United Funds was organized to circumvent many of the problems and pressures resulting from individual campaigns. But an exaggeration of zeal among at least some United Fund enthusiasts has brought on fresh problems and intrusions.

United Funds, which in 1962 took in $525.1 million, receives most of its contributions from employees, employers and corporations. Employees give through payroll deduction plans and provide the bulk of United Fund contributions. The coercive element is present, as it cannot help but be when employees are asked to "volunteer" donations for a system of philanthropy strongly backed by management. In numerous instances personnel managers have shoved pledge cards at new employees, suggesting not only that they sign but indicate the amount of contributions expected. *Newsweek,* in a roundup on Detroit's famed Torch campaign, noted that the automobile companies, in competition with each other for fund quotas as well as car sales, hand out a list of "fair-share" contributions. In 1963 a $5,200-a-year man was expected to give $31.20. A Detroit resident is quoted as saying, "One man I know hasn't had a salary increase since 1955, because he won't give a nickel." There was some bitterness about the campaign's "triple-hit"—solicitations at work, at home and at school. Basil O'Connor, president of the National Foundation, had a point when he stated, a few years ago, "Charity is supposed to be private. It should have no bearing on a man's employment."

From the beginning, United Funds, with its theme of federated charities and its slogan of "Give Once for All," incurred the wrath of the large, independent health agencies which were determined to retain their autonomy. Claims and counter-claims, accusations and counter-accusations, have for the past dozen years turned the charity field into a battleground.

The result has been predictably unfortunate. Neither side has won but confusion and bitterness reign supreme. The National Foundation has consistently refused to have anything to do with United Funds. The American Heart Association and American Cancer Society tried United Funds and found it wanting for their purposes. The break has not been clean. When the American Cancer Society declared that henceforth all local chapters would have to withdraw from United Funds, some 30 chapters withdrew from the American Cancer Society instead and elected to remain with United Funds. So did some 200 local chapters of the American Heart Association; they were not expelled from the national organization but new Heart chapters are not allowed to join UF. Similarly, there are chapters of other national health organizations, as well as the Red Cross, within and without United Funds.

Compounding the competition, many United Fund chapters raise money for cancer, polio or whatever other disease is represented by a group that has refused to join United Funds. The rivalry occasionally helps some recipients. Henry Webber, associate executive director of United Funds, explains that a medical school might get grants from both United Funds and the American Cancer Society, as well as from the U.S. Government, the community, corporations, and individual contributions.

The rivalry has been less than pleasant in terms of community relations. In plain language, the milk of human kindness has been curdling dreadfully. Some United Fund officials have publicly asked the people of their communities to stop giving money to the national health agencies. Volunteers have been pressured into abandoning their efforts on behalf of the National Foundation and other independent agencies. As *Good Housekeeping* reported, "With the lines of combat sharply drawn, the family identified with the less popular of two competing causes in a particular neighborhood may discover that continued loyalty to the cause means strained relations with employers, neighbors, business associates, customers, and even relatives."

The pressure on the public has not been eased by the fact that the health agencies have a history of feuding among themselves. An official of the Muscular Distrophy Association admitted to this internecine warfare when he said, "I think there is duplication of effort. There is splintering of organizations because of internal politics." In 1953 the Muscular Dystrophy Association itself suffered an intramural upheaval when a number of its chapters broke away to form the National Foundation for Muscular Distrophy (now known as the National Foundation for Neuromuscular Diseases). A hassle is presently in progress between the American Cancer Society and the Leukemia Society. In at least one community, ACS proponents urged people not to volunteer for the Leukemia group.

The unfortunate din from the philanthropic arena reached the ears of the Rockefeller Foundation, which proceeded to underwrite a survey of the situation. Under the direction of Dr. Robert H. Hamlin, the surveying committee in 1961 issued a report that praised the voluntary health and welfare organizations for their dedication and service. It then went on to blast them for holding on to internal machinery that

161

"has become antiquated, patched up, and at times jealously self-centered." It pointed out that the terrific competition "has resulted in the failure of too many voluntary agencies to present a fair, balanced picture of their activities."

The report suggested that "it does not take over 100,000 voluntary agencies, in the opinion of many," to provide private health and welfare services in this country, and that "a better job could be done by a smaller number and greater joint effort." The report concluded by recommending the establishment of a national commission on voluntary health and welfare agencies, and uniform accounting and reporting procedures throughout the health and welfare field.

It should surprise no one that the Hamlin Report was severely criticized by the American Heart Association, the National Tuberculosis Association and other voluntary agencies. By 1963, efforts were still being made to set up a commission. Though meetings among representatives of the various fund-raising and charitable institutions have been held, no drastic reform has yet taken place. Incidentally, in 1945 the Rockefeller Foundation sponsored a study similar to the Hamlin one. Results of both studies were practically identical.

In the intervening years the dilemma faced by the thoughtful donor and the eager volunteer has deepened. On the one hand he realizes that there are vital community and national needs that can only be met through his active, voluntary participation. And he wants to participate. On the other hand, he runs into an atmosphere of commercialism that too often seems to say, "Get his dough—it's for a worthwhile cause—and to hell with him."

The fund raiser quoted earlier, who said that people would not throw money over the transom, was partially correct, of course. As a fund-raising official for the Children's Aid Society of New York has written in another connection, "Few of us are capable, very often, of the pure charity which is the greatest of all virtues." Noting that regardless of how meritorious the cause, some people will object to it, she added that "moral pressure in various forms is utilized in all kinds of organized fund-raising."

Moral pressure, yes. But what kind and how much of it? Does it have to include the coldblooded approach best suited to sell toothpaste? Is the individual to be denied even the privacy to make up his own mind whether he wishes to act nobly? Are we not getting into pressures that contradict voluntary giving?

These are difficult, painful questions—and it does not seem as though the fund-raising industry as a whole has tried to answer them. The prevailing attitude has been neatly summed up by one professional of many years' standing with whom I discussed fund-raising and intrusion. He said he is tired of people who whine. He said, "Whenever we come up against a whiner we find that he does little or no contributing. It's the quiet guy, the one who sits in a corner of the room and says nothing, who is the generous contributor."

In the final analysis, of course, the public has something to say about it all. The public is in control—or should be—and the present situation has come about in part because it has not been forceful enough in exercising that control.

It is not enough to give, if that giving is nothing more than a conditioned response—if it is unaccompanied by thinking, planning and checking. It is up to each of us—as individuals—to reject some of the more intrusive techniques, to refuse to be drawn into acrimony unworthy of any philanthropic enterprise, to be more than just contributing machines, to really involve ourselves in—and find out about— the causes that meet our interest. Finally, it is up to each of us to recognize that we have the right to say "No" as well as "Yes," for no matter the extent of our generosity, it is impossible for one person to give to all. Only by putting some privacy back into giving can we get some spontaneity and joy out of it.

14. In Defense of Privacy

> *The right of the people to be secure in their persons, houses, papers and effects, against unreasonable searches and seizures, shall not be violated. . . .*
> *Portion of the 4th Amendment to the Constitution*

WILL ALL THE prying, digging, peering and poking into our "inviolate personalities" finally render privacy obsolete? A couple of generations hence, will some automated society look upon privacy with the same air of amused nostalgia we now reserve for, say, elaborate eighteenth-century drawing room manners?

One shudders to contemplate an affirmative answer. With the passing of the eighteenth century merely went the extreme graciousness of that particular age. With the complete annihilation of privacy would go the last vestiges of individuality. Throughout modern history man—and in particular Anglo-Saxon man—has bitterly resisted any attempt to encroach too greatly on his privacy. He knew the alternative was a society in which neither the heaviest clothes nor the thickest walls would keep him from remaining naked and exposed. A society in which his every word, thought, emotion and action became public property, to be used and assessed without his knowledge by forces beyond his control. A society in which—regardless of the number of rooms in his house—he would have no room to really call his own where in private he could replenish himself to become again a vital and creative member of his group. He knew that nothing was more devitalizing and degrading to his stature as a man than to live with the constant fear that somebody might be looking over his shoulder or barging into his quarters.

He knew instinctively that the ultimate fate of privateless man is to turn into a robot ready—even eager—to embrace a communal way of life in which his leaders make all his decisions for him. Thus Anglo-Saxon law erected towering safeguards to protect the individual's privacy against the dangers of an overly inquisitive and tyrannical government— safeguards embodied in the Fourth Amendment's proscription against improper searches and seizures.

There is an irony here. Our regard and respect for the meaning of the Fourth Amendment has not diminished one iota through the intervening years. Few of us would look on apathetically if the police crashed into our houses without proper search warrants. Yet it does not occur to us to grant the Fourth a degree of relevance in situations unforeseen by the framers of the Constitution. The framers could hardly have foreseen the astonishing advances that have been made in the technology of intrusion. They could not have known that in time private power-aggregates—labor unions, political pressure groups and (mainly) the business community— would make as much of an impact on the individual as his government did. One can only conjecture what they would have said to wiretapping, bugs in the company washroom, professional blacklisting clubs, or hidden TV cameras perpetually casting their nerveless gaze on corporate employees.

But one thing is sure. If we were to apply their moral yardstick to some of the more flagrant invasions of privacy currently in vogue, it would make a mockery of the Amendment.

Obviously not all of the intrusive practices described throughout this book are equally virulent. But even the relatively inconsequential ones must be viewed with apprehension when the more serious ones are so readily accepted. With every violation of our privacy—big or small—we grow more accustomed and more tolerant to intrusion generally. Ashley Montagu has called this "an increasing callousness" to "the transgressions upon our being, the violations of our privacy, and the infringement of our right to be alone with ourselves whenever we choose." He went on to observe, "This is life as we know it, and the harder it grows the more hardened do we become to it."

A New York sociologist offered me a striking example of this hardening process. He told of a study in which behavioral scientists not long ago secreted tiny microphone-transmitters in the bedrooms of married couples in a college housing project. The idea was to find out just how similar people are in their lovemaking. It's beyond our purview here to make value judgments on sociological research—though this particular study hardly seems earth-shattering enough to call for such an offensive research method. The point is, however, that the couples involved didn't think it so offensive. Once the field work was completed they were advised what had been done, promised anonymity, and requested to give their permission for the researchers' use of the tapes. Instead of screaming invasion of privacy, every last couple gave its permission. Maybe the unwitting participants in the study felt the harm had already been done. Much more likely, they were so sophisticated—that is, so inured to baring body and soul—that they saw little amiss.

The increasing callousness with which we accept the most blatant intrusion is appallingly evident in an area in which a deep and abiding respect for privacy ought to be taught above all else—the schools. Yet this should hardly overwhelm us with surprise. As Edgar Z. Friedenberg has so accurately noted in his book, *The Vanishing Adolescent*, "Our schools are a precise expression of our culture."

One scarcely knows where to begin the list of privacy violations perpetrated on our schoolchildren. Martin L. Gross makes it clear that a majority of junior and senior high schools now give, without obtaining parental permission, personality tests designed to lay bare each student's psyche and expose the most secret parts of his personality. Incredibly enough, whole classrooms are now also required to fill out "problem checklists." As Mr. Gross explains it, "Scores on a child's worries and fears, on sex, dates, Mom and Dad, fights over the car, family finances, even teen-age menstruation—once considered the exclusive province of parents—not only become part of the child's school record, but are inevitably bandied about" by some school authorities.

A number of secondary schools in the U.S. have installations of a device appropriately called, by a sociologist acquaintance of mine, "bitch-boxes." More precisely, they are loudspeakers with tiny microphones secreted inside. They enable the principal of the school to talk to—or eavesdrop on—any classroom at will. Needless to say, sooner or later the secret is out. Then both students and teachers go through the schoolday knowing that at any given moment they may be surreptitiously audited.

Still other schools have adopted the closed-circuit TV system as a way of keeping tabs on the boys and girls. A few years ago an upstate New York high school installed such a system in its study halls. The principal could look at a telescreen in his office and observe what the unattended boys and girls were doing. In his estimation, they were doing fine. "Now there is no daydreaming," he said.

Plagued by increasing hordes of inquiring government and private security investigators seeking information on former students who are now job applicants, some colleges and universities make little effort to preserve the confidentiality of their student records. Both files and transcripts of grades are open to anybody who can prove a legitimate interest in the information, without the student's permission. Other schools strive to strike a balance between the students' right to privacy and the community's "need to know." But the very fact that investigators ask questions about political affiliations, social and religious outlook, behavior patterns and the like, inhibits the attitudes and actions of contemporary students who look ahead to their own days as job applicants. They tend to play it safe; to be more guarded and less apt to express themselves spontaneously. Their realistic fear of loss of privacy results in a loss of their opportunity to use the school years for experimentation, for trying and discarding new ideas. Professor Louis Hacker points out that the relationship between student and teacher ought to be nothing less than privileged—like the relationship between patient and doctor. Notes an ACLU study headed by Dr. Hacker:

"The society which subordinates academic freedom to security precautions faces many more problems than it solves." Educators have discovered that students are also becoming reluctant to use school facilities they might have need for— particularly psychiatric services—because disclosure of the information later on might keep them from getting a job. Dr. Saul Stone, clinical psychologist on the staff of Brooklyn College, told me that many students who come to him for therapy begin their sessions by saying, anxiously, "Can we keep this off the record so it won't get into the files?"

The end result of the free-and-easy approach to student privacy is easily predictable. Enduring intrusion throughout their entire scholastic history, young people are not likely to depart from their citadels of learning inspired to a lasting respect for other people's privacy. More likely, they will simply join the ranks of those businessmen who have an exaggerated interest in their employees' and customers' private lives. Or join the public payroll with a similar disregard for individual privacy as balanced against community needs.

Nothing here should suggest we lead our lives in morbid secrecy. There is often the unfortunate tendency to equate privacy with secrecy. This misses entirely the point and meaning of both words. Doing something in private implies a free choice about revealing the act. Doing something secretly means driving it underground. When an individual's total personality—not merely his talents and abilities—is hired, and he feels he must conform or else, his tendency is to turn private acts, attitudes and modes of life into secret ones. Or to give them up altogether because somebody in authority might disapprove. Either way, the squeeze is put on him. On the one hand, he feels guilty about something he is perfectly within his rights to think, feel or do. On the other, he plays it safe and knows (if only unconsciously) the self-contempt that follows. And, of course, fear of criticism leads him to a fear of exerting his full potential on the job.

In a 1957 speech, former U. S. Senator Herbert H. Lehman focused on the "play-it-safe" pattern. He said, "A typical training pamphlet of the General Electric Company advises all professional employees, as part of their basic code of conduct, to avoid taking an interest in 'controversial' questions. And there is some evidence that many college students who aspire to work for these corporations are taking this advice in advance. Some members of some faculties in some colleges and universities have suggested this attitude as the correct one for those who want to 'get on' in the great bureaucracies which have grown up in the corporate world."

Not to suggest that the corporate world has a monopoly on this restriction of the individual's privacy to live his life as he pleases. Some unions, church groups, boards of education and other institutions are similarly possessive about their constituents.

Privacy neither is—nor can be—an absolute condition. As the population grows, society becomes more complex and our interdependence increases—a set of circumstances that forces us to make public more and more of our private affairs. Precisely this fact of life should lead us to guard ever more zealously what privacy we still have left. It's a question, then, not of absolutes but of degree. Putting it another way, too often a justifiable invasion of privacy becomes sheer exploitation by overstepping the bounds of necessity and propriety. For instance:

Market research is necessary to the production of effective advertising, but is it proper to make a habit of taking secret films of housewives shopping?

The gauging of an insurance applicant as a good or bad actuarial risk is a necessity, but is it proper to go behind his back and use neighbors' reactions in part as the gauge?

The checking of credit is necessary, but is it proper to use information proffered in good faith by the credit applicant for personnel reports, jury checking, mailing lists or any other purpose not under the heading of credit?

The elimination of pilferage, malingering, and other forms of employee-created losses is a necessity, but is it proper to use paid spies on a permanent basis as a way of fingering potential trouble?

Questions such as these assume even greater urgency when we consider the frightening inventions in the technology of intrusion and their possible adaption to commercial investigative purposes. In the summer of 1963 a news report disclosed that Westinghouse is developing a machine able to "write" thoughts. There is no reason to doubt that by matching brain wave patterns with specific words, sooner or later a device that translates thoughts into words will be developed. The notion that such an instrument would ever be used as part of a pre-employment screening process (to name one way it could be used) may seem absurd. But why not? The applicant could be directed to "think" out the responses to his employment questionnaire; though perchance he might concentrate on evasions or lies, the truthful answers hovering in the back of his mind would always be there to give him away. Why not, indeed? The notion becomes less absurd upon reflection: some thirty years ago, who would have guessed the indiscriminate uses to which the polygraph is now put?

Already on the market is the Alertor, an automatic device whose purpose, as *Newsweek* has succinctly put it, is to watch the men who watch the automated machinery. This device surveys an automation technician's movements inside a specially created magnetic field monitored by an antenna laced into a floor pad. If his movements correspond to the working pattern under surveillance—that is, if he is doing a proper job —all's well and good. If he deviates from the pattern an alarm goes off, summoning his superior. This latest gift to Big Brotherhood was recently installed in eighteen diesel locomotives belonging to a Midwestern railroad. The reaction of the engineers on those runs can be gauged from the fact that the railroad, according to *Newsweek*, refuses to be identified.

The scales are further tipped against privacy by the irreversible trend to the use of computer systems in storing and handling personal data. Banks, insurance companies, telephone company offices, credit card companies, some personnel departments in industry, airline and railway companies, the Internal Revenue Service, Social Security and Selective Service have all become heavily dependent on the various types of automatic data-processing equipment. The impact of this trend is twofold. First, much of the programming calls for each person filed to be reduced from name to number. In essence, this means practically all of us. This has stirred the imaginations of some computer-happy scientists. They have already envisioned the day when every person will be tagged from birth to death with *one* identifying number that would serve all needs, governmental and private—even, if technical details can be worked out, as a telephone number. And to make sure that nobody could ever forget or escape his number is the crux of two other ideas. These may not do much for privacy or individuality, but in an era that prides itself on practicality, they have the virtue of being admirably nononsense: 1) tattoo that identifying number on some inconspicuous spot on each newborn babe; 2) implant in baby's skin a miniscule radio transmitter (complete with lifetime batteries) that would, upon electronic demand, emit the identification number in code. Suggestions like these may sound far-out enough to smack of science fiction; one only wishes they were.

Though less obvious and less dramatic than numbered

man, there are other dangers to privacy inherent in computer systems with their fantastic concentration of personal information. The data could easily be drawn on and used in ways not originally intended. A skilled programmer could tamper with the information. Most important of all, entirely separate data-processing systems could be pooled, shared, fed into each other. This is already being done between the Internal Revenue System and the Social Security System. Your income, tax payments, bank transactions, insurance purchases, credit card transactions, employment background information, telephone calls, flying trips and other private data could conceivably all be consolidated some day to keep a running and detailed account of your activities, available in moments. If this ever occurred it would be the death-blow not only for privacy but for the very democracy upon which it nourishes. To be sure, no one has suggested such a consolidation of data (at least publicly). But there is a potential danger and—because so often privacy invasions tend to be creeping and progressive, therefore taking place relatively unnoticed—that danger should be viewed with the utmost seriousness. Some scientists are beginning to do just that. In January 1962, Dr. Richard W. Hamming of the Bell Telephone Laboratories publicly voiced his concern over the potential dangers to privacy inherent in the increasing storage of personal records in computer systems.

The entire problem of individual privacy—its erosion and exploitation—deserves considerably more attention than it has been getting from legislators, lawyers, educators, scientists, psychologists and sociologists, the clergy and the press—all those whose responsibility it is to bring moral values to society. It deserves increasing attention from all of us because we are all involved—that is to say, in one way or another we are all victims.

Surprisingly little on the subject has appeared in books and magazines. William Zelermyer's *Invasion of Privacy* dealt with a variety of illuminating law cases in the realm of privacy and affirmed privacy as a fundamental human right. In 1962 a book by attorneys Morris L. Ernst and Alan U. Schwartz, *Privacy: The Right To Be Let Alone,* traced the evolution of the law of privacy in cases involving mass media and mass communications. Both books make excellent reading on the legal aspects of privacy, though they do not concern themselves with invasions that might not come under tort law.

In the popular magazines a rash of feature articles has dealt with electronic eavesdropping. Some articles have touched peripherally on corporate invasions of privacy. A prominent one in 1963 was Vice Admiral H. G. Rickover's "The Decline of the Individual," which appeared in the *Saturday Evening Post*. During the past 20 years less than half-a-dozen popular magazine articles dealt at all with the meaning of privacy in our lives and the tragedy of its loss to modern man. Just one did so comprehensively. This was Ashley Montagu's "The Annihilation of Privacy" in the March 31, 1956 issue of the *Saturday Review*. More discussion of this caliber is needed in the popular press. Needed too is more public awareness of the many ways in which our privacy is being exploited; as you have seen, much of what goes on is secret in the most literal meaning of the word. It may sound hackneyed to refer to an aroused public opinion; however, what more effective weapon is there to stop the exploitation from growing more acute? It is interesting to note that several states took action to tighten up their wiretap laws *after* the hue and cry that followed a number of widely publicized wiretap scandals in the early 1950's. Public opinion may influence state legislatures to ban lie detectors for industrial purposes, as has already happened in Massachusetts.

One hopeful portent is a special study being conducted by the New York City Bar Association's Committee on Science and Law. The Committee hopes to formulate legal proposals that would effectively deal with the pressures technology has placed on privacy. Other bar associations should conduct similar studies or explore other ramifications of our vanishing privacy.

Another way of curtailing the more extreme privacy violations—electronic and other—would be to increase the hazard of civil suits. Persons whose privacy has been invaded should do something about it. True, privacy suits are often costly and time-consuming, and, given the present condition of our privacy laws, the chance of winning is slight. Thus, it is up to attorneys to persuade the courts to take a more favorable view of privacy. In some instances the courts already have. A significant decision was made by the West Virginia Supreme Court in 1958. The Court ruled that a woman whose landlord had bugged her apartment (to see whether she was respectable) was entitled to recover damages for this invasion of privacy. Referring to this case, Professor Alan Westin noted that lawsuits against "business, union or social eavesdroppers would provide a deterrent in that particularly sensitive area—the pocketbook."

There have been significant lawsuits won in other areas. When a meat-packing house employee in North Dakota was fired and denied his pension after a lie detector test indicated that he had pocketed sheep-feed funds, he sued for damages and was awarded $36,000. John Henry Faulk, a radio and television entertainer, won a $3.5 million libel suit against Aware, Inc., a private screening service that had blacklisted him and ruined his career. (The award has been appealed.)

Ordinarily, shadowing, the questioning of neighbors, the making of background checks, the planting of TV cameras or undercover agents—all such intrusions in the personal sphere are not actionable. The problem of their use belongs in the moral, not legal, sphere. Here, too, the victim is not always helpless. Late in 1963, the AT & T installed a hidden camera in a men's washroom in one of its New York City buildings to trap a pervert who had been defacing the walls with obscene drawings. The device snapped pictures every 7 seconds of everyone who entered the washroom. When employees accidentally discovered the camera they protested and their union local threatened a strike. Nobody held any brief for the pervert, but—understandably enough—nobody wanted to use the washroom knowing they would be photographed. The camera was removed.

We all of course have a freedom of choice about our own actions. Some Americans *have* declined lucrative jobs because they resented the batteries of psychological or lie detector tests. Contrary to what examiners say, a substantial number of those who declined did so out of principle, not because they had something to hide.

Our freedom of choice is certainly self-evident when it comes to revealing to strangers information about our neighbors. When the affable investigator comes to the door, we should remind ourselves that we are not just being helpful, not indulging in a bit of mild gossip—we are informing. (There are exceptions: aiding law enforcement officials during the investigation of a serious crime; cooperating with private investigators when the subject of the interview is aware of the interrogation.) Too, we might look upon privacy not only as an inalienable right but as a commodity, a piece of property. When we reveal the intimate details of somebody's else's life without his knowledge or permission we are giving away something that simply is not ours to give— *his* attitudes, *his* actions, *his* conversation, *his* conduct—*his* "inviolate personality." This notion may not seem so far-fetched when we consider that the exploiters of privacy profit by the information either in selling or using it; therefore it is in a very real sense property to them.

What is needed most of all is not legislation or lawsuits or attitudes culled from the immediate situation, but the return to a fundamental respect for privacy—our own and other people's. This is something neither law nor lawsuits can bring about. Yet how can the respect come back? And how soon? Not swiftly, perhaps, and not easily—but through a steadily growing awareness of what privacy means to us as individuals, and as a nation; what its loss would effect; and what the encroachments upon it are.

A final defense of privacy might well come from the lips of William Pitt, who stood before the British Parliament in 1776 and, in a speech against the use of general warrants, uttered one of the most eloquent pleas ever made on behalf of the individual's right to be let alone: "The poorest man may, in his cottage, bid defiance to all the forces of the Crown. It may be frail; its roof may shake; the wind may blow through it; the storm may enter; the rain may enter; but the King of England may not enter; all his force dares not cross the threshold of the ruined tenement."

Times have changed; a person's cottage is understood now to be not only his physical house but the intangible elements of his inner self; the threat comes not only from public officials but from a horde of private exploiters whose intrusions actually exceed those of the Government. And so, ultimately, nothing has changed: the threat is here, it is real, and it bids us all to stand defiant on our thresholds.

Appendix

SOURCES

CHAPTER 1
Mr. Rickenbacker on the census: *National Review,* May 21, 1960.
Mr. Zelermyer's comment from: *Invasion of Privacy* by William
Zelermyer, Copyright © 1959 by Syracuse University Press. Truth
Verification report: *San Francisco Chronicle,* February 13, 1961.
William Faulkner on privacy: *Harper's* Magazine, July 1955.

CHAPTER 2
Mr. Black on ACB of A files from: *Buy Now, Pay Later,* by
Hillel Black, Copyright © 1961 by Hillel Black. Reprinted by
permission of William Morrow & Co., Inc. Teamsters and U. S.
Government checking on prospective jurors: *The New York Times,*
September 11, 1958.

CHAPTER 3
Mr. Dooley's speech reported by: *National Underwriter,* October
20, 1961. Mr. Zelermyer, *op. cit.*

CHAPTER 4
Mr. Eldot's advice to executives from: *Getting and Holding Your
Executive Position,* by Leon Davis Eldot, © 1960 by Prentice-Hall,
Inc. Mr. Gross on psychological testing from: *The Brain Watch-
ers,* by Martin L. Gross, Copyright © 1962 by Martin L. Gross.
Reprinted by permission of Random House, Inc. Remarks made
by Temco Electronics security officer: *Business Week,* November
10, 1962. Use of Bible during security interviews: *Industrial Security,* April 1958. Mr. Rauh's testimony given to *Subcommittee on
Constitutional Rights,* 84th Congress, 2nd session. Wire inspector's
story from: *Security, Civil Liberties and Labor Unions,* an AFL-
CIO pamphlet by Harry Fleischman, Joyce L. Kornbluh and Ben-
jamin D. Segal. Comment on D & B security reports appeared in:
The Reporter, February 10, 1955. Report on the American Security Council and other far right movements appeared in *Men of
the Far Right,* by Richard Dudman (Pyramid Publications, 1962).
New York Post article on ASC by William Haddad; reprinted by
permission of *New York Post,* Copyright 1958, New York Post
Corporation. Prof. Hacker's remark: *New York Times Magazine,*
November 17, 1963.

CHAPTERS 6 and 7
Generally favorable article on commercial lie detection: *Business
Week,* June 18, 1960. Highly critical article on same: *Harvard
Business Review,* November-December 1962. Case involving young

Texan from: ACLU press release, February 5, 1962. Case reported by U. of Va. professors: *American Journal of Psychiatry*, May 1963.

CHAPTER 8
Use of bugs and wiretaps by business and industry from: *The Eavesdroppers* by Samuel Dash, Robert E. Knowlton and Richard F. Schwartz, Copyright © 1959 by the Pennsylvania Bar Association Endowment. Reprinted by permission of Rutgers University Press. Quote on shoppers from: *The Investigator's Handbook*, by Arthur Liebers and Capt. Carl Vollmer, Copyright © 1962 by Arco Publishing Co., Inc. Mr. Walsh on handling thieves: *Industrial Security*, April 1962. *Fortune* quote and anecdote from October 1961 issue, courtesy of *Fortune* Magazine. A small portion of this chapter appeared in *Climax*, May 1962.

CHAPTER 9
Harvard IE study published as: *Competitive Intelligence*, by Burton H. Alden, et al (C.I. Assoc., 1959). *Harvard Business Review* poll appears in its November 1959 issue. *Fortune* quotes from May 1956 issue, courtesy of *Fortune* Magazine.

CHAPTER 10
Mr. Dash on telephone company laxity: *Coronet*, March 1961. Mr. Williams on Costello's wiretapped phone from: *One Man's Freedom* by Edward Bennett Williams, Copyright © 1962 by Edward Bennett Williams. Reprinted by permission of Atheneum Publishers.

CHAPTER 11
Mr. Keats's tale: *Horizon*, January 1963. Independent Telephone official's quote: *Wall Street Journal*, February 26, 1963. Detailed account of FS & R creative-drama technique: *Sponsor*, April 29, 1963. Mr. Shils on electronic eavesdropping from: *The Human Meaning of the Social Sciences*, edited by Daniel Lerner, Copyright © 1959 by Meridian Books, Inc. Reprinted by permission of Meridian Books, Inc.

CHAPTER 13
Muscular Dystrophy official's quote: *Wall Street Journal*, October 11, 1960. Mr. Carter on fund-raising from: *The Gentle Legions* by Richard Carter, Copyright ©1961 by Richard Carter. Reprinted by permission of Doubleday & Co., Inc. Children's Aid Society quote from: *Reporter of Direct Mail Advertising*, May 1962. Mr. Church on fund-raising methods from: *So You're Going to Raise Funds*, by David M. Church (Nat'l Publicity Council for Health & Welfare Services, Inc., 1957).

CHAPTER 14
Mr. Gross, *op. cit.* Mr. Westin on wiretaps: *Commentary*, April 1960.